Life Expectancy

A Memoir

Rachael Maddux

Cover design by Rachael Maddux. Cover image: *Mount Hecla Iceland*, by Charles Hamilton Smith (1776-1859).

Copyedited by Rebecca Bowen.

Back cover photo by Lindsey Lowe.

ISBN: 979-8-9923566-4-9 (paperback), 979-8-9923566-5-6 (ebook)

[1]

For my family

"It seems to me that one ought to rejoice in the *fact* of death—ought to decide, indeed, to *earn* one's death by confronting with passion the conundrum of life."

— James Baldwin, "Down at the Cross"

"I'm so excited. I'm so excited. I'm so scared!"

— Jessie Spano, *Saved by the Bell*

Contents

A Note

This book is primarily a work of memory, one written in good faith and with deep appreciation for the vagaries of human perception. Some names have been changed.

The Beginning

Once upon a time, I was out at a bar with some friends on a Saturday night. It was still summer, but it wouldn't be much longer. We were all in our twenties, but we wouldn't be much longer. We were drinking something called The Wasp: whiskey and honey and lemon, fancy salt and pepper. My friend Kate was talking. "I've been having a lot of anxiety about death lately," she said. "I think it's because my grandmother just died. I don't know, I've never really thought about it before." Outside the light was golden and inside everything was warm and moving slow. But Kate's words jangled in my head. I was totally flummoxed. Neither sober enough nor drunk enough for anything resembling an earnest reply, I found myself slumping out across the table, my elbow parting a sea of half-full glasses, voice low like I was imploring her to recount some illicit rendezvous: "Tell me what *that's* like."

My friends all laughed and I laughed too. The conversation stumbled elsewhere and we ordered another round. The rest of the night passed in a cheery haze. After we said our goodbyes, I walked home with the last of the season's cicadas rattling in the trees. But part of me was snagged on that moment: Kate's confession, my reply, everyone laughing, over and over again. I went to bed thinking about it. I woke up thinking about it. To realize, as an adult, that you'd never really thought about death before—I really did want to know what that was like. She might as well have said, *I've been breathing a lot lately. I don't know, I've never really converted oxygen to carbon dioxide before.* How else could you live?

That night at the bar, it was September 2012. I was two months away from my twenty-eighth birthday. I was the oldest daughter of an art teacher and an asphalt emulsion plant manager, born and raised in the renaissance years of what had once been called the dirtiest city in America— what would later be called the most churchgoing city in America—in the muggy, mountainous bottom-right quadrant of the world's most powerful country during the victory lap of the twentieth century. When I was a kid, my parents and sister and I watched *America's Funniest Home Videos* together most Sunday nights, and witnessing strangers falling off bicycles and taking baseballs to the crotch was largely the extent of my exposure to human suffering. My existence was one of rounded edges and narrative predictability. Now I was married and living in a bigger city, and my husband and I were talking about thinking about wanting to get a dog, and we were just laughing anytime someone asked if we wanted to have kids, and even our ambivalence felt like following a script.

But death is predictable too. And so it crept in, had always been creeping in, even into this copacetic existence. That's what it does. And I took notice, had always been taking notice, because that's what I do. It's been there for as long as I can remember, that hard little fact-of-all-facts: One day I will die, and so will everyone else. Back when I was a child, selfish and self-orbiting, I assumed that everyone else knew this too. Nobody really talked about it, not in any direct way, but nobody really talked about plenty of other things I understood as real and universal: money, farts, s-e-x. Everyone knew what I knew about death, I thought, and everyone felt how I felt about it, which was mostly afraid—mostly, but not completely. I was desperate to forget about death, was thinking all the time about how to forget it, and of course this made forgetting impossible. But I was also more than a little intrigued, which made my inability to forget kind of thrilling. I was always looking away then looking back out of the corner of my eye. I wouldn't recognize it for many years, but this maddening loop of repulsion and attraction was also the mode of the world at large, which always seemed to be denying death's existence, or at least its relevance, while producing an overabundance of evidence to the contrary. Death was somehow unreal and omnipresent, fundamental yet unspeakable. I thought of my fear of death—the fear, everyone's fear—like a skeleton: natural, essential, holding us all upright. Without it, weren't we all just floppy sacks of gristle? How else would a life know what shape to take?

I was a child, it seems, for a very long time.

Then it happened: that night at the bar, my friends, our Wasps. The casual revelation of the absolute wrongness of my life's most fundamental assumption. It happened and then it kept on happening, rolling over me in the days and weeks and years to come, a cascade of disorienting, reorganizing truths: that I was not bound to all of humanity in a collective, silent preoccupation with the inevitability of death. That I was tied up—pretty well tangled, actually—in a long string of my own personal apprehensions and misapprehensions. That it was possible for something to be knowable, and known, and still not understood, not for a long time, maybe not ever. But I wanted to try, I wanted to grasp as much as I could: Where had it come from, this knowledge of death? How had it grown in me, how had it grown me, how had it shaped and been shaped by the life I'd been living—my steady-plodding, predictable life? And was it possible that this life was less generic than I believed it to be —something particular, if not quite peculiar? The life of a young and then increasingly less-young person who has never once forgotten that one day she is going to die.

"Tell me what *that's* like," I said to my friend that night, a joke that wasn't a joke, a tipsy command that splashed back in my face. What was it like, to grow up that way—a life free of death, free of the fear, free of the strange joy too? I still don't know. That's someone else's story to tell. But this one, it's all mine.

Apprehensions

I would like to start by describing the moment I first learned about death. I would like to tell you when it happened and how it happened and how it felt and what I did next. But I can't. For all the times I've tried to summon it up from the depths of my memory, so far I've only failed. I used to wonder if maybe I couldn't remember the moment because there was no moment to remember, maybe I couldn't learn about it because I always already knew it, maybe I was born a bald little baby with it already in my head—an instinct, a reflex, a predisposition. Most likely, it did happen and I just forgot. Even more likely, it was never a single moment, more like a gradual accumulation, a mass that grew so slow and steady it came to feel like an essential part of me before I even realized it was there.

But we have to start somewhere, so how about this: I arrived on a bright blue November afternoon, my mother and father's first child. It was 1984. They drove me home from the hospital in their orange Volkswagen Bus. The bus had a busted heater and every time we left the house that winter they entombed my carseat in blankets, certain I was going to freeze to death; they were less concerned, apparently, by the possibility of suffocation. Spring came and I was still alive but they traded the bus for a Dodge Caravan anyway.

I walked early, talked early, started hoarding memories early. In the morning there was sunlight around my window shade, a platoon of stuffed animals at the foot of my bed, my mother's face above me with her big glasses and black curls. In the backyard, tulip poplars glowed green and orange in the sun. Late afternoon, when I thought everything was settled, my father would swing through the front door, his soft plaid shirt with M&Ms in the pocket to bribe my skeptical hugs. His beard against my cheek, warm parking-lot smell. In bed at night, I gathered up everything I collected about the day and set about piecing it together, just in time for it to all fade back into darkness.

My sister arrived when I was nearly three. At birth Sarah was already half my size, round and pink with round blue eyes. I was gangly with brown hair so sparse it looks gray in our grainy eighties snapshots. My one advantage was that my sister had nothing to her name that hadn't once been mine. I'd already grown in that body, slept in that crib, forced the washing of all those clothes. It wasn't enough. I could feel her watching me. Once, left alone with her in the living room, I dared to get close—close enough for her to reach up, weave her fingers into the thin hair at my temple, and yank my face down to hers. She breathed ominously into my ear, releasing her grip only when our mother heard a cry and called out to me from the kitchen: "Rachael, don't hurt the baby!"

It was strange to remember that I had a name. It was strange that one day my sister didn't exist and then she did, and one day I hadn't existed either. Sometimes something flashed in my brain and I had to stop whatever I was doing to think about how I was a person and what did that mean?

Sometimes I felt like I was watching myself from above, drawn out of myself like a rubber ball pulled away from its paddle, until the moment passed and I dropped back down again. Bounce bounce bounce.

* * *

We lived in the suburbs of Chattanooga, Tennessee, in a 1970s split-level in a subdivision full of 1970s split-levels, the streets named on a loose Revolutionary War theme, on land I would one day learn had been stolen from the Cherokee. Inside was wood paneling, blue carpet, beige walls my mother had stenciled with assorted pineapples and folk-art filigrees. Above our basement stairs hung a little wooden sign I couldn't read until one day I could, and it said, "Bloom where you are planted." Down the stairs was an old dog named Buster. He had wild white curls, a black nose, black eyes. He had lived with my mother since she was in art school in Florida, and she told my sister and I all about his glory days running up and down the beach, chasing seagulls, rolling in dead fish. Now he was deaf and blind and spent most of his time sleeping or looking for somewhere to sleep. He regarded me coolly, but he liked my sister. Her first word was my name and her second was his. She built Milkbone skyscrapers that he destroyed like an arthritic Godzilla. When he barfed, our mother would place a chair over the pile until she had time to clean it up. A reminder, a warning.

Next door lived our neighbors Don and Lydia. Their house was ours in mirror image, right down to the Dodge Caravan in the driveway, only they had a motorcycle too. Don wanted to fly planes but he drove a truck instead. Lydia was a cashier at K-Mart. They weren't old but their children were grown up and gone. In December, Lydia would bring us presents. One year, she crossed the yard with a K-Mart Christmas bear tucked under each arm, "1989" embroidered on their right feet. The next year, she arrived carrying two wrapped boxes and I saw stars like she'd whacked me upside the head with them. A bear was good but a box was better, a box could be anything.

We sat down in the living room, Lydia and my mother and my sister and me. Sarah unwrapped her gift slowly and with infuriating tenderness, the way she did everything. I ripped into mine. Under the wrapping paper was a pink box with a thin plastic window, and inside was a plastic baby: eyes scrunched shut, arms and legs drawn up around its tiny body, pink mouth puckered into the shape of a soundless wail, looking way too alive and way too dead at the same time. Something shot through me, a bolt of primal disgust. I screamed, I threw the box, and I ran—up the stairs, down the hall, and into my bedroom. I hurled myself into bed and buried myself under the blankets and pressed my body into the mattress like it might swallow me up and take me far away, away from the terrible baby in its terrible little box and the terrible world that made such a thing possible.

After a while, my mother appeared. She stood in the doorway, then sat on the edge of my bed. She rubbed my back for a while, the way she always said I liked it when I was a baby. She said, "Can you come downstairs and tell Miss Lydia you're sorry?"

"No," I said. "I don't want to lie."

"Well," my mother said, and I don't remember what else. Maybe she left me alone. Maybe I followed her back downstairs anyway; I seem to recall Lydia crying, and my sister crying, but that might have just been what I imagined, or a memory of what I was told later. I felt embarrassed to have become so upset, and to have upset everyone, but also unsure what else I could or should have done. It was the most horrible thing I'd ever seen in my life.

Eventually I did retrieve the baby in its box from the corner of the living room and begrudgingly introduced it to my other toys. They all had names but I never named the baby. I wasn't sure what I was supposed to do with it. It had a little diaper with tiny Velcro tabs. I took its diaper off and put it back on again, and I moved its arms and legs in their sockets, and I stared at the weird pink hole of its endlessly screaming mouth. Otherwise it was impossible to play with, poseable but inconsolable.

Not soon enough, if you'd asked me, I started kindergarten. My elementary school was a red-brick building with an American flag out front and an Exchange Club Freedom Shrine in the lobby and framed Norman Rockwell prints up and down the halls. Every morning, a voice in a green box on the wall asked us to please stand for the Pledge of Allegiance. We stood with our hands over what we thought were our hearts. Then the green box told us what was for lunch. Next to the green box was a green bell and when the bell rang that meant recess. Every day I waited for that bell to ring, but once it did I couldn't remember why. Outside, all the other kids seemed to know what to do. They ran around and screamed and glommed together into games as if they were receiving directions on some frequency I couldn't tune myself into. I mostly wandered around, from the four-square court to the monkey bars, always pretending I was on my way to somewhere else.

One day I realized I could see across the street. There was a church there, red brick like my school with a little white steeple. And next to the church was a strange swath of green grass, pierced here and there by scraggly trees and gray stone slabs: a cemetery. I knew what a cemetery was because at home I had a tape of *Casper the Friendly Ghost* cartoons. I knew that when you died they put you in a box and the box went into a hole in the ground and then you became a ghost, and every night when it got dark you and all the other ghosts floated up from your graves, laughing and howling, then flew off to the city to gather the screams of the living. I liked Casper because he wasn't like that. He didn't want to scare anyone, he just wanted a friend. When he found one, a little fox, some hunters shot it dead. Casper was so sad but then the fox became a ghost too but death still seemed lonely. I didn't want it.

I hated the cemetery and I couldn't stop looking at the cemetery. Even when I turned my back I could still feel it, like it was looking at me too. None of the other kids or the teachers seemed to notice, or if they did, nobody mentioned it. Sometimes I wondered if I was the only one who could see it. Sometimes I would see people in dark clothes huddling under a green tent, sometimes a yellow backhoe and a mound of red dirt. Sometimes I would see a new burst of flowers left behind on a grave and in the days and weeks to come it would get tumbled over and kicked around by the wind, finally coming to rest in the ditch, the petals and wires carried off by birds for their nests or to choke on.

Every day when the bell rang at the end of recess it was a shock. Some days everyone's voices, even my own, would unite in a swell of mass indignation. We'd only just arrived, or we'd been out there for hours—either way, it was never enough. Our teachers would just shake their heads and wave us back inside. They knew the world was operating on timetables we wouldn't understand for years. The most we could grasp were these cruel base facts: When it's time, it's time. When you're called up, you go.

Strange—my parents had once been children, too. My mother was also born in Chattanooga, and her parents still lived in the house on the hill where she grew up with her three brothers. Her oldest brother, Mike, had two sons but they lived in California, useless to me. Her youngest brother, Tom, had a tarantula named Babydoll. Her middle brother, Frank, and his wife lived across town and had three daughters: Claire and Lucy, who were younger than me and therefore belonged to my sister, and Marie, who was mine.

Marie and I counted once, and she was born two months, three weeks, and two days after me. It was weird that I'd ever existed without her. She was the only person who reliably seemed to understand anything I thought I had to say about the world. I had a ponytail and she had a bowl cut and our primary shared interest was suffering. We hid from our sisters and drew detailed cross-sections of hospitals packed with broken bodies in complicated traction. We rushed our Barbies into surgery and diagnosed our Zoobilee Zoo hand puppets with terminal diseases. When they died they looked just like they always did.

I went to the emergency room for the first time when my arm popped out of its socket while I was dancing with my grandmother. I knew not to talk about it—I'd read *Madeline*, I knew how people got jealous when bad things happened to you—but I did tell Marie. She had been to the emergency room, too, when she couldn't breathe because she had too much snot in her nose. Upon my second visit—the night I danced across a rough patch of hardwood floor basement and lodged a two-inch splinter deep in my heel—I worried I'd disrupted our balance. Soon after, though, Marie went camping with her family and got a burning hot marshmallow stuck in her eye and we were equal once more.

But for how long? There were so many ways to get yourself hurt. On *Sesame Street*, a girl broke her arm roller skating and got a thick plaster cast. On the news one night, a boy got experimental surgery after chopping off his finger with an axe. I watched *Pollyanna* over and over, holding my breath every time Hayley Mills started climbing that tree with her doll in her teeth, bracing for the scream and thud. I read a story about kids with bad hearts who lived in hospital beds hooked up to machines. Sometimes in bed at night, I lay with my eyes closed imagining I was floating in the dark surrounded by beeping things keeping me alive. Sometimes I fell asleep and woke up with a mouth full of blood and a sticky wet face and a dark blotch spreading across my pillowcase, terrified to move, certain that if I turned my head the rest of my blood would come pouring out of me. Instead I lay still as if truly paralyzed, yelling and yelling until my mother appeared and steered me into the bathroom. There she sat me down on the toilet lid and tipped back my head, gripping a washcloth to my nose, tossing it into the sink when it was soaked, red turning to pink when the water ran through. I loved it when my mother took care of me but sometimes it also made me sad. I understood in a distant way that her services wouldn't always be available to me. One day she had been a child and now she wasn't. I was a child and one day I wouldn't be either. I wasn't sure what would happen in between. It seemed like too much time and not enough. So I just sat there with my arms hanging at my side, sleepy and helpless, until the bleeding stopped and my mother wiped my face and sent me back to bed, hot metal tang at the back of my throat.

* * *

As Buster the old dog got older, no longer even charmed by Milkbone architecture, Sarah decided that she wanted a cat. My mother said she could have a cat if she caught one herself. We got goldfish instead. One each, scooped from a tank of hundreds by a Walmart employee who assured us the ones floating along the top were just sleeping. At home, my father plopped the fish into a glass bowl with gravel the exact shape and size but not taste of Fruity Pebbles. My mother set the bowl on the sideboard in the living room. Sarah's fish was bright orange—classic. She said its name was Goldiefishie. My fish was silvery-white. I don't remember what I called it, only that I detested the name "Goldiefishie." It hurt my teeth to even think the word.

"When do they sleep?" I asked after a while, thinking about the tired fish in the Walmart tank.

"Oh," my mother said. "Whenever they get tired, I guess?"

"Yeah, I guess," I said, turning back to the fish and their hopeful nibbling at nothing.

Sometime later, months or weeks or just days, we came home from church one Sunday and I saw that my fish was finally asleep, its belly pressed against the side of the bowl. Relief hit me first—it must have been so tired!—and then the sickening dread. Those fish at Walmart hadn't been sleeping. I'd known it then, deep down, and now I knew it again. I didn't scream this time, didn't throw anything, but I did run. Up the stairs, down the hall, and into my bedroom, where once again I tried to press myself through the mattress into some other dimension, and once again that proved to be beyond my abilities. I'm sure my mother came up to console me and coax me back downstairs; I'm sure, once again, I refused.

Later, when I did emerge, I made myself go look at the bowl on the sideboard. My dead fish was gone. Nobody told me what became of it, and I never asked. Goldiefishie swam on, alone with its stupid name.

* * *

I could always tell when Don and Lydia were going out riding on their motorcycle from the racket that preceded their departure: the stubborn dry yammering of Don kicking the bike awake, the grimy burble of it idling as they loaded themselves up, the impatient wet rip of the engine mounting and fading as they disappeared down the road. One morning, a few minutes after this symphony, an unusual coda: our ringing doorbell. When my mother opened up, Lydia was standing on our porch covered in blood.

"We hit that curve over on Pine Ridge and spun out on some gravel," she said as my mother pulled her into the house. "Ron skidded clear across the road, went under a fence—" She held out her hands, red and wet. Her face and arms were red, her legs were red, blood was running down her legs and soaking into her white socks and her white hi-tops. A red drop hit our blue carpet and turned black. My father called 9-1-1 from the yellow phone on the kitchen wall then ran outside, and in a second I saw the blur of his blue Datsun truck speeding away. My mother steered Lydia to the bathroom and I followed. From the safety of the doorway I stood and watched my mother sopping up all the blood, the pile of ruined washcloths in the sink. She pulled out her first aid box and the sight of it made me woozy, the rubbery smell of old Band-Aids, the mysterious snakebite kit. "Can you walk?" my mother asked after a while. Lydia stood and managed a shuffle, like a cartoon mummy.

Soon as our van turned onto Pine Ridge, I saw the lights: red and blue strobes weird in the mid-afternoon sun.

14

People in black and blue uniforms prowled around. My mother parked on the shoulder and steered Lydia into the crush of paramedics, Sarah and I waited, still buckled into the backseat. Out my window I could see the offending patch of gravel, the motorcycle on its side in the ditch, the gnarled metal coil of chain-link fence. I could see the green lawn rutted down to dirt by Don's projectile body. I couldn't see him but I knew he had to be dead, knew his body was splayed out in the yard somewhere. I didn't want to see it but I couldn't stop looking.

But when my mother and father emerged from the crowd, they were shaking their heads and almost laughing. My father got into his truck and drove toward home. "Ron's pretty beat up, but he's going to be fine," my mother said to my sister and I in the rearview mirror. "Lucky son of a... duck."

I didn't believe her until a few days later when I saw him for myself, waving to us across the yard. His arm was in a sling and he had scrapes and bruises all over, but he was alive. It didn't matter. After that, every time our van rounded that corner on Pine Ridge I held my breath. I always expected to see Don's crumpled body in the corner yard, and I always expected us to hit the same patch of gravel and go skidding out to join him, spiraling out in a low spray of sparks like a dud firework on the Fourth of July.

* * *

I had this growing sense that I needed to keep my wits about me. In our backyard I had to stay busy picking roly-polies out of the sandbox and clearing around the rotten dogwood stump where my elves lived. Anytime I looked up I might glimpse the backside of the house behind ours, where two high windows and a resting ladder formed a giant, grimacing face. Worse was the dense thicket that grew along the ditch at the bottom of our hill, where the snakes lived. I'd never seen them before but I knew they were there and I knew they wanted to get me—why else would there be a snakebite kit in my mother's first aid box? But they couldn't get me if they couldn't see me and they couldn't see me if I couldn't see them. So I kept my head down and made sure to always sit on the swing facing uphill. Sarah didn't seem to know what I knew. She swang facing the snakes and the danger. She was always swinging. She would swing and cry. I never knew what she was crying about, and years later, when I finally thought to ask, she didn't remember.

One day my mother picked us up from school and drove us to a birthday party. She stood with the other mothers as we ate cake and swatted at a low-hanging piñata. Then she drove us home. Three steps into the house she dropped her purse, turned back to us, and dropped to her knees. "Girls," she said, her eyes behind her glasses suddenly level with our own. "There's something I need to tell you." Her voice sounded a way I'd never heard it sound before. My leg-bones went wobbly. "Girls," she said again. "Buster died this morning. He hadn't been feeling good for a long time, but he's not hurting anymore. He's buried out in the backyard. If you want, I'll show you where and you can tell him goodbye."

I'm sure Sarah began to cry then, her face a pink mess, and our mother stretched out her arms, and she ran into her embrace. But I was already gone.

After a while, like always, my mother appeared in my doorway. "Are you sure you don't want to go see?" she asked. "Your sister wants to."

I was sure. For a while I was sure I would never leave my room again, let alone my bed, but I did. For a while after that, I was sure I would never go into the backyard again, but then I did that too. Back to the sandbox and the elves and the swings, back to the terrible ladder face and the ditch full of snakes, and now a new danger too: I didn't know where the dog was buried so he was buried everywhere. I minced around like I was always about to step on his grave, like it posed some threat, like he was a landmine and not an ancient poodle mix. Sometimes I looked at my sister, blonde curls falling down over her face as she bent to some small task, and I thought, *She knows. She knows and I don't.* Sometimes I wished she didn't know. Sometimes I wished she'd tell me. Even now, I don't know what I wanted: for me to be brave like her, or her to be scared like me.

The Far Side

Occasionally I feel certain that I can remember my own baptism. "You were a *baby*!" my mother said when I told her this once. "You could barely hold up your own head!" But I swear I can still feel the weight of the congregation's eyes on me as I was carried down the center aisle in my little white dress, then the shock of the dark nave giving way to bright lights as I was tipped over the stone basin and marked as Christ's own forever. I admit that it does seem far-fetched, but I cling to it anyway. I appreciate that my earliest memory of organized religion is a lovingly held delusion.

In this recollection it's my grandfather, my mother's father, who baptized me, and this, at least, is true. Some insurance auditors, when they retire, take up golf; my grandfather became a non-stipendiary priest ordained by the Episcopal Diocese of East Tennessee. He baptized my sister too, and he'd married my parents years before, my mother in ivory lace, my father still woozy from his bachelor party. We called him Papa but at church everyone called him Father Landis. My grandmother, who we called

Nannie, was not called Mother Landis, which I thought was unfair, but she didn't seem to mind.

My parents took my sister and I to church some but not all Sundays. It was the same every time, which of course was half the point. We would walk through the big red doors, through the cool, dim narthex and into the dark nave, and Nannie would be sitting in one of the long wooden pews, which we'd scoot down one by one to join her. If I sat all the way back against the curved wood, my feet dangled inches above the floor, an expanse of small blue tiles that in my mind became water the second I broke contact. The copper pipes of the organ towered up along the far wall, and when they began to hum everyone stood to welcome the slow parade of acolytes and choir and clergy down the aisle. I stood too, the water turning back to tile as soon as my feet touched down, and craned my neck until I saw Papa: white hair, white robes, arms around a big red book.

The book contained a story that we heard more of each week. The telling of it seemed to have been going on for a long time, possibly since before I was born, and there were big chunks missing, and it was all out of order, but I got the gist: God lived in the sky and was in charge of everything. He made Earth and all the people on it, and then he made himself a son named Jesus to go down and make sure we were all okay, like how my mother sometimes sent me outside to see what in the world my sister was doing. God and Jesus wanted everybody to be good, and if you were good, when you died, you got to go to Heaven. But it hadn't always been like that. For a while, God was up in Heaven all alone. Back then, when you died, you just disappeared. But then God made Jesus and Jesus died and God felt bad so he had Jesus come up to Heaven with him, and then he thought, *Well, isn't this nice?* So he invited all the people he made on Earth to come up to Heaven when they died too.

But they had to be good, because otherwise Heaven would get crowded with bad people and then it would just be Earth again, except in the clouds. If you were bad then you went down to Hell, which was also forever, but with flames.

The problem with people, which God seemed to have forgotten even though he made us, was that we were never all the way good or all the way bad. So you couldn't know whether you were going to Heaven or Hell until you were already dead. After you died and were buried in your casket then you floated up into the sky and waited in line outside the Pearly Gates. When it was your turn, Saint Peter would look up your name in his big book. If he saw your name, the Pearly Gates creaked open and boom, you were in Heaven. But sometimes there was a mistake. Sometimes Saint Peter would realize that you weren't going to Heaven or to Hell because you weren't supposed to be dead at all. He'd make a joke about it then send you back to Earth, ha ha ha. Nobody talked about this at church, but it happened all the time in the *Far Side* cartoons Papa taped up next to his word processor at home, so I figured it must be true. And if the *Far Side* was true then maybe my old friend Casper was true, and the red-faced preacher in *Pollyanna* whose comb-over flapped as he yelled about fire and brimstone, and actually, the more I thought about it, the more everyone seemed to have their own ideas about what was going on. There were all sorts of ways to get into Heaven, or only one way, or no ways at all. Chattanooga was full of churches and every Sunday they were full of people like us listening to people like my grandfather saying different versions of the same things, or different versions of different things. But afterwards we all went out to lunch at Arby's or Blimpie or Cracker Barrel just the same.

Once you got to Heaven—once it was "your time," as I

heard grownups say, as if the rest of your life belonged to someone else—you got a white robe and a halo and you became an angel. You could talk to other angels as much as you wanted. Every angel got their own cloud. You could use your cloud to float down to Earth and spy on all the people you used to know, like they did in *The Family Circus*. But you weren't allowed to talk to them and you had to be sneaky about it. Was a ghost an angel someone on Earth saw when they weren't supposed to? Maybe. Some angels were babies, but they weren't dead babies. God made them too. He thought about sending them to Earth, but they were so cute, he kept them all to himself. Heaven was up in the clouds, but not the ones we could see from Earth, the ones above those. You had to get up pretty high. Sometimes I followed the far-away shape of an airplane until it disappeared into the clouds, and I thought maybe planes could get high enough to go to Heaven, straight through it even. God and Jesus and all the angels could see the plane and the passengers through the little windows, but the people on board couldn't see them, they had no idea. Whenever you saw a big pile of fluffy clouds and then the clouds broke apart and the sun beamed through, that was God peeking down at you. My mother said that's what she thought when she was little, and it sounded right to me. God up there waggling his fingers at us like we were babies in a crib. When I saw God up in the clouds, I remembered how far away Heaven was. I knew it was real and that one day I might go there, like college or Universal Studios, Florida. But there was so much I had to do first.

To someone on Earth, God would seem gigantic. But once you were an angel in Heaven he would seem regular-sized. It would be like how Papa seemed so large during church but at home, out of his priest clothes, he wore grass-stained khakis to check the chlorine levels in the swimming pool. Like Papa, I figured God would talk about gardening and politics and quote Monty Python, that he would be in charge but not bossy. He would have thick white hair, too. And all the angels up there with him would be good forever, not because they already were, but because they wanted him to love them, which he already did, in ways they'd never understand. I wanted desperately to be good. It seemed easy enough at church but it was hard in the whole rest of my life. I kept forgetting. I wouldn't clean my room, or I would talk back, or I would make my sister cry. I hated it when my mother said my middle name or when my father frowned, tilted his head, and breathed out his nose. But sometimes it wasn't enough. I guess God knew the threat of his disappointment wasn't enough, either, so that's why he made Hell.

One day at school, at recess, two blonde girls beckoned me over to the far end of the playground. Their hands were dirty. They'd cleared away all the pea gravel from around a fist-sized rock. One girl whispered to me, "Hell is under that rock." The other one said, "If you pick it up, you can see the Devil." I wondered how small the devil must be to fit under that rock, and I tried to pick it up and see for myself, but it was stuck in the ground. The two blonde girls just laughed at me. I wanted to tell them my grandfather was a priest and he knew all about it, whatever it was, but I just laughed too.

If Saint Peter didn't see your name in his book, if you'd been mostly bad, then a trap door opened underneath your feet and you fell right down into the flames. I couldn't picture what it was like to burn for even a little while, let alone forever. It must have been hard to imagine for all the people who wound up there too, or else they would have tried harder to be good. On Earth when I was bad, the worst my parents would ever do was swat my butt and send me to my room. But I liked my room. It had all my books and stuffed animals and my big wonderful bed. My sister wasn't there trying to do everything I did or playing with my toys wrong or crying for no reason. My mother had painted some butterflies flying over one wall, a big rainbow across the other, and a tall sunflower growing in one corner. And wasn't that what Heaven was supposed to be? Everything good, nothing bad, just your ideal scenario all day long forever? It was nice, for a while. I played or read or watched the sun make patterns on the ceiling, which looked like icing on a coconut cake. But then beyond my shut door I could hear my sister running up and down the hall, my father laughing, my mother opening the linen closet and the flump of clean towels on the shelf. They were living without me, perfectly happy.

At church when Papa said, "Let us pray," I knew what I was supposed to do. I put my head down and looked at my hands. Sometimes he said the prayer alone and sometimes all the grownups read along from the blue Books of Common Prayer they pulled from the pew-back in front of them, and before I could read too I mumbled along with everyone, sure the sounds coming out of my mouth had to mean something. At home, my parents and sister and I said the same blessing before dinner every night: *God is great and God is good, let us thank him for our food, amen.* As if He and not my mother had set the stew going in the Crock Pot that morning. In books and in cartoons, rosy-faced children were always kneeling by their beds, hands clasped, heads bowed, filing their daily reports with God. I wondered if my parents were being negligent by not requiring me to do the same. Once or twice, just in case, I tried it for myself. After lights-out, I slipped out from under the covers and arranged myself like I thought I was supposed to be. But it was all wrong: My mattress was too tall for my elbows to rest on, the floor was hard under my knees, plus I didn't know what to say. There was plenty I wanted, toy-wise, but that was Santa's domain. Maybe I was supposed to thank God for all the ways I was good and apologize for all the ways I was bad. But when I tried I couldn't remember which was which.

Sometimes in bed at night, when I wasn't imagining myself hooked up to beeping machines in a hospital room, I thought about all the people buried in the cemeteries in their coffins, all of them laying on their backs in the dark too. I thought about Hell, where I didn't want to go, and I thought about Heaven, which I wasn't too excited about either. I didn't know anyone who was dead and I didn't want anyone I knew to die. But how could Heaven be perfect if no one I loved was there with me, except Buster who never liked me and the fish whose name I couldn't remember? I maybe would have rather burned. When my thoughts drifted in that direction, I felt like I did sometimes when I slept over at Marie's house, a shiver around my heart when I thought of my bed in my bedroom, empty without me. Homesick, I guess, but I was already home.

Flocks

Cookeville, Tennessee, is a large small town on the Cumberland Plateau, and my father grew up on the edge of it, in a place called Dry Valley. When he was born his parents lived with his father's parents in a big farmhouse, and when his brother was born they moved into a little house across the road, and when his grandfather gave up the farm his father took it over and they moved back into the big house. Tobacco, cattle, Tennessee Walking Horses. By the time I was little, my grandparents, who we called Nana and Grandaddy, had sold the farm and moved closer to town and into another big house, this one with tall white columns and black shutters, a rolling yard full of old trees and gumdrop hedges, and a name: Pigeon Roost.

I was the first grandchild on that side of the family, my sister the second and last. The drive was two hours up from Chattanooga, lined with kudzu monsters in summer and, in winter, gnarled fangs of waterfalls against shorn-off mountainsides. My stomach dipped and turned along with the Dodge Caravan up the twisty road to their gravel driveway, always a little nervous on the approach, even though what happened next was nearly always the same. We'd go in through the side door, booby-trapped with a skein of sleigh bells. Nana would emerge from the kitchen, apologizing for the Crisco on her hands and leaving big red lipstick smudges on our cheeks. Down the hall, in the den, the TV would be set on a Vols basketball game or an Andy Griffith rerun and two old men sat on either side of the fireplace. The man in the red-leather armchair was Grandaddy, who would fling his arms wide and holler, "Come give me some sugar!" Sarah and I would oblige with quick kisses on each cheek, his skin loose and stubble-rough. The man in the hickory twig rocking chair was Unk, Grandaddy's brother, our father's uncle, and he would call us over to trap us in a hug so he could pop his dentures out at us, first the top then the bottom then both at once, perfect white choppers with pink resin gums, making us scream and squirm loose and run from the room, still screaming.

Unk was so often at Pigeon Roost when we arrived that for a time I thought he lived there too. In fact he lived over in Dry Valley, alone in the little house where my father had grown up. He had no children, had never been married. He was a diabetic with a sweet tooth. When he took my sister and I to Baskin Robbins at the Cookeville Mall he'd tell us to order whatever we liked, but we always wanted what he was having, which was always two scoops of Sugar-Free Jamocha Almond Fudge. He drove a blue Crown Victoria with seats upholstered in blue velour you could brush dark one way and light the other. He wore the same outfit every day, brown pants and a brown shirt. His actual name was Fred and he was the namesake of my father's brother Freddy, which I thought was fitting because they were both short and bald, and meanwhile my father and Grandaddy were both tall and bald. Smaller and taller versions of one another, like Sarah and I, or so we were told: the "spittin' image" of one another, people said, though people also told me I was the "spittin' image" of my mother and Sarah was the "spittin' image" of our father, and our mother and father looked nothing alike, so I wasn't sure how any of this was possible. I thought I just looked like myself.

In Chattanooga, my mother's side of the family made a tidy, three-generational pyramid with my five cousins and my sister and I on the bottom, my parents and aunts and uncles in the middle, and my grandparents on top. In Cookeville, it was all upside down, Sarah and I the lone children under a thick plinth of grownups. There were people we called cousins who weren't our cousins, aunts who weren't our aunts, and up there people said "aunt" like they said "ain't," like, "She ain't my aint." There was Nana and Grandaddy and Unk; and my Uncle Freddy, who—like my mother's brother Frank—had also married a Susan; and there was my grandmother's sister Aunt Lucy, and her husband Uncle Sonny, though his real name was Garland; and Nana and Lucy's cousin Billy Harper, who they called by his first and last names even though he was nearly a brother to them and there were no other Billys he might be confused with; and quite a few men who shared my father's name of Ralph; and assorted Buds and Buddys and Bobbys, for whom last names were infrequently given; and two women, one named Aunt Dimple and the other Aunt Dimp, one with gray hair and one with white hair, one named after the other though I could never remember which, or even whose aunts they were. These people all had five, six, seven decades of shared history to their confounding names. In the den, or on the screened porch, or at the long dining room table, I'd hover around the edges of conversations, trying to understand, but I often couldn't tell if they were talking about something that happened yesterday or fifty years ago, and there were all these other people—Aunt Janie, Uncle Herschel, Mammy, Ga, Granny

Hill—who I sensed were dead now but seemed as alive to these old folks as they themselves were to me.

How was it possible that they had all been young once? It was weird, but I could believe that my parents had been children; they still had parents of their own. But with these others, all I could imagine were wrinkled faces and bald or gray permed heads on child-sized bodies. This, despite photographic evidence all over the house: a colorized portrait of tiny Nana with pink cheeks and yellow ringlets, a blurry snapshot of Grandaddy and Unk as toddlers, slouching on a front porch in coveralls like two old farmhands. The walls of Pigeon Roost were scaled with photographs and paintings, mostly of long-dead family and the houses they'd lived in, and I liked to walk from room to room staring at them like a tourist at a museum. Nana and Aunt Lucy and Billy Harper went to Scotland one summer and came back with coats of arms of all the family's families, which Nana framed and hung outside the dining room: the Comyns, the Carrs, the Jareds, the Lowes. Before Tennessee we'd been in Scotland and Wales, maybe even in America before Columbus if the tales of Prince Madoc were true. When Tennessee had its bicentennial, the Governor's office sent a stack of certificates with gold seals, one for each of my grandparents' ancestors listed among the state's First Families. Nana framed and hung those too. Sometimes I would stand and stare up at the display, over-whelmed by all this proof that we belonged here—this state, this country, this world—and had for so long.

Pigeon Roost once seemed big enough that I thought it must be a mansion and that, since it was theirs, my grand-parents must be very rich. I'm still not sure of the house's relative size—perhaps I was just small, and it was just old and built on a hill—but I do know, now, that my grandpar-ents did not own it. The house had once belonged to

Grandaddy's uncle, a man everyone called Uncle Bob Lee, a taciturn local businessman and fox hunter who died around the time my grandparents sold the farm in Dry Valley. His own children inherited the place, but they'd moved out of Cookeville years before. So my grandparents moved in, with Uncle Bob Lee's tools still hanging in the garage, his wife's childhood toys in the attic. They paid rent and took care of the place. It was never theirs at all.

* * *

Back at home in Chattanooga, my parents and sister and I moved from one 1970s subdivision to another 1970s subdivision. My parents traded in the Dodge Caravan for a Plymouth Grand Voyager. Every year at school, I was in a new classroom with a new teacher. Every year I made friends with a new girl whose father's job transferred him again the next summer. Every few months my clothes no longer fit, my shoes no longer fit, my small teeth fell out and bigger ones grew in. My hair kept growing and needing to get cut. Once the lady at Fantastic Sam's gave me feathered bangs but then those grew out too. Everything was always changing. But up in Cookeville the world of Pigeon Roost stayed put, I thought, like the Peach Fuzz creatures and the balsa-wood furniture in the dollhouse Nana kept for Sarah and I at the top of the stairs, activated only by our presence.

This became a hard illusion to maintain when people started to die. Aunt Dimp was the first. September 1993; I was almost nine. When my father told me I felt sad, because he seemed sad, but mostly I felt bad that I couldn't remember if she was the silver-haired one or the white-haired one. On the drive to what I thought would be her funeral, I thought about the gray stones across from my elementary school, the green tents, the red piles of dirt. I was in third grade and my class had recess on the new playground behind the red-brick elementary school but I still thought about the old playground and its view of the cemetery all the time. I'd never known anyone who was about to get buried. I'd never known a person who died at all. I thought we were driving to Cookeville, where I thought she lived; instead we were driving to Nashville, where she actually lived. We went to her house, or the house that had been hers when she was alive. Inside, every small room seemed to lead into yet another small room and I entered each one of them holding my breath, certain her body was around every next corner. But all I saw was a bunch of vaguely familiar grownups and tray after tray of small sandwiches. All the side tables, dresser tops, couch arms, and chair backs were draped with white crocheted doilies. I imagined Aunt Dimp's body, wherever it was, also draped with a white crocheted doily. We left before I found her. We left before anyone could explain to me that this was not a funeral, she'd been buried that morning, she was gone twice over now. On the way home, we stopped at the Nashville Parthenon and for years to come I would insist that I'd seen the real thing.

A year later, another day in September, my parents called my sister and I into the living room. They were both sitting on the loveseat. Sarah and I sat on the floor. "Girls," my mother said, then turned to my father, who shook his head, so she went on. "Unk died," she said, in the same strange voice she'd used to tell us about Buster years before, nearly the same words too: "He was sick for a long time, but now he's not anymore." I knew it, he shouldn't have had the Jamocha Almond Fudge, even if it was Sugar-Free. I crawled under the coffee table and pushed my face into the carpet and I didn't move for a long time. A few days later, we came in through the side door at Pigeon Roost and the sleigh bells jangled like always, but everyone inside the house was quiet. In the living room, Grandaddy sat in his red armchair across from the empty hickory-twig rocker. My father's old friend Richard's wife Paula appeared after a while and Sarah and I went with her back to her house. Richard and Paula had two daughters too, and a shag-carpeted basement, and a Super Nintendo. We played *Super Mario World* until our parents appeared at the top of the landing: my mother in a black dress, my father in a suit. They had been to Unk's funeral without us. For a moment I felt tricked, then jealous, then relieved.

* * *

Grandaddy was sick by then but nobody knew until December. He'd been sick for a while, maybe a year, maybe five, maybe the whole ten I'd been alive. When we went up to Cookeville for Christmas, the big bed from the guest room upstairs was now down in the living room, and Grandaddy was in it all the time, and the couch was upstairs where the bed used to be, and the TV/VCR cart had been wheeled in from my grandparents room. All week my sister and I lay around up there watching *The Sound of Music* and rented tapes of *Dinosaurs* while downstairs the grownups did whatever they were doing. Sometimes I would dare to go downstairs to get a snack from the kitchen but I always kept my head down and ran past the den's open doorway, determined not to get sucked into whatever was happening in there, because what was happening in there, though nobody said it out loud, was that my grandfather was dying.

December became January and one afternoon a mass of starlings descended on Pigeon Roost's front yard. They arrived as a black cloud in the bleached gray sky, then fell to cover the grass on either side of the long gravel driveway.

When there was no more room on the ground they began to fill the old trees and the gumdrop hedges, everything with a branch as far as I could see. The noise was constant—thrumming, rustling, chittering—but the constancy was delicate. One tap against a windowpane, one jostle of the side-door's sleigh bells, and the flock would explode and swarm above the house like smoke. Soon enough they'd drift back down to earth, like they wanted to leave but couldn't, trapped by a force no one could see.

When our winter break from school was over, my mother drove my sister and I back to Chattanooga and my father stayed in Cookeville. I planned to pretend as if this was a typical arrangement if anyone at school asked me why, but nobody did, nobody seemed to know at all; an insult, and a relief. One day that week we stepped off the bus and saw Nannie and Papa's blue Dodge Horizon parked in our driveway—strange. Inside, our mother was sitting with her parents at the kitchen table, all smiling big, flat smiles. "Why, hello there," said Papa, as if we were the ones making an unusual appearance. I knew it then, but I didn't start crying until the words came out of my mother's mouth.

Back up at Pigeon Roost, I found that some attempt was under way to fill my grandfather's absence with food and plants. The refrigerator was packed with casseroles, and the living room, where the Christmas tree still stood, was crammed with overflowing vases and wreaths on tripods and potted tropical plants. An unknown someone had sent Nana multiple jumbo-sized samplers from See's Candy all the way out in California. Freddy was calling him the Candy Man. "That Candy Man's making a move on you, Mama," he teased. When another box arrived he said, "That Candy Man don't know when to quit!" Nana set out the sampler boxes all around the house and I took a piece every time I passed one, and then another if the first was nougat. I made myself go into the den. The bed was back upstairs; the couch was back downstairs. On a side table I saw a copy of that morning's *Herald-Citizen* open to the obituaries. Grandaddy's was the biggest of them all, top of the page with a big black-and-white picture. I sat down and read it. He was sixty-five years old. He'd been a farmer, like I knew, but he'd also been Putnam County Road Supervisor, and campaign manager for two would-be Tennessee governors, and founder of a paving company, and a one-term President of the National Walking Horse Breeders and Showers Association of America. The Aunt Dimp who died two years earlier had been his older sister. The other Aunt Dimp was his actual aunt. She was listed among his "survivors," as if there'd been a shipwreck. Among the survivors were "two granddaughters, Rachael and Lauren"—my middle name instead of Sarah's first name. For a moment I felt bad for her. Then I noticed where I was sitting: Grandaddy's red armchair, the seat still sunk in the shape of him. I dropped the paper and left the room.

Sarah and I escaped to the yard. Someone had given us each a finger puppet, a chipmunk and a raccoon, and we'd accepted them like the consolation prizes they were clearly meant to be. We draped ourselves over the lowest branches of the magnolia tree and watched the cars come and go. "Look, there's Nannie and Papa," the chipmunk said to the raccoon as the blue Dodge Horizon came up the driveway. A strange sight, like characters from one movie appearing in another. They waved at us and we waved back and I thought about how unfair it was that my mother had two parents but now my father had only one. Then I thought about how none of my grandparents had any parents left at all. There seemed to be some point in a person's life when it was more unusual to have parents than to not have them. I didn't know when that point was, exactly, but I had a hunch it had something to do with having children. Once you became a parent, your own parents became vulnerable somehow. Adding meant subtracting. I looked at my sister, deep in conversation with the rodent on her fingertip, and wondered which of us had pushed Grandaddy out.

The night before the funeral, my mother sat us down and told us how it would work. First there would be a service at some place called the Hooper-Huddleston chapel, then everyone would get in their cars and drive out to the cemetery in Buffalo Valley, where Grandaddy grew up, where he would be buried, and finally everyone would come back to Pigeon Roost to be together and eat some more. She presented this agenda with frank neutrality, the way she might explain an afternoon of errands to be run. But I loved running errands, and I hated this. "You can come if you want, but you don't have to," she said at last. "It's up to you, my girls." Sarah said she wanted to go. I made my choice too. Or perhaps I'd made my choice years before—the day I ran from my mother telling us Buster had died, the day my sister went out back to see the grave and I hid inside. These were, I thought, just facts: My sister was someone who could do this, and I was someone who could not.

In the morning, my father's old friend Richard's wife Paula came to pick me up from Pigeon Roost. It was a Wednesday and her daughters were at school, so I played *Super Mario World* alone in the basement, my little shag-carpeted refuge. Yoshi and I hopped around, grabbing coins and stomping mushrooms, and I tried not to think about why I was there, but trying not to think about it was just another way of thinking about it. I was a bird flying over-head the whole scene. I could see the line of black hearses snaking through the cemetery, the rows of gray tombstones slumping against one another in the soft gray earth, everyone in their black coats huddled against the wind, all their black umbrellas converging into a spiny mass that conveniently obscured my imagined view of the casket being lowered into the ground. Was Grandaddy in Heaven yet? I'd never thought to ask how long it took to get up there. But if he was, then he could see me down on Earth. He could see that I wasn't at his funeral. Could he see himself at his funeral? Could he see himself in the casket? That's what I'd been most afraid to see. I didn't want him in a box. I wanted him where he belonged: in the red armchair, at the end of the dining room table, in the saddle on a big brown horse. Anywhere except where he was going to be forever.

When Paula drove me back to the big house that afternoon, the yard looked like the parking lot at the county fair, cars parked up and down the long driveway and in rows down the lawn to the street. I steeled myself before going through the side door, knowing the sleigh bells would announce my arrival. I could picture everyone turning toward me with their hollow faces and red eyes, a stunned silence falling over the conversations they would be having about all the horrors they had witnessed, if they could even speak at all.

The bells did ring, but nobody heard them. The house was full and bright and warm, like a party—certainly more festive than our Christmas had just been. There were more casseroles out and more boxes of See's Candy, and everyone was standing around eating and talking and laughing. Even my father and Freddy and Nana, when I saw them through the crowd, were smiling at whoever they were talking to. The house was packed with uncles and aints and cousins, some familiar, most strangers. They all gasped at the sight of me and slapped their cheeks in shock that I was no longer the bald baby they'd met a decade earlier. They all said they knew how much my grandfather loved me and how sad I must be and they were praying for me, they were all so sorry, they couldn't believe he was gone. I guess I couldn't either. I kept looking around for him, listening for his laugh.

I found Sarah among all the tall bodies. We pilfered chocolates and retreated to a far corner of the living room jungle. In my exile, I'd imagined my sister bundled away inside one of the hearses, tucked between my parents, all of them gray-faced and weeping on the long ride without me. She had seemed so small in my mind. I'd pictured her dressed in a black coat and hat that I knew she didn't even have. Her actual coat was purple and she wasn't so small anymore. She was seven, older than I was when the cemetery first entered my consciousness, older than I was when I ran away from the dead fish and the dead dog. She was the same as me and so different. We sat among the peace lilies and the parlor palms and ate our Ms. See's, each bite tentative until the lack of nougat was confirmed. She told me about the preacher who gave Grandaddy's eulogy and how everyone knew he was reading from the *Herald-Citizen* obituary when he said, "his granddaughters, Rachael and Lauren." When that happened, she said, Freddy leaned over and poked her in the ribs and they both laughed. Laughed right there in the middle of the funeral! How was that possible? How was it allowed? She told me how hard the wind blew through the cemetery when it was all over and everyone was walking back to their cars. "All the umbrellas turned inside out!" she said, and I imagined the black domes folding back on themselves, straining against their fragile joints, then flying away in a burst of black wings.

Seen and Unseen

One Saturday that April we drove to Pawleys Island, which was barely an island, more like a scab halfway up the shin of South Carolina's coast. The Waccamaw and Winyah people lived there first, then the colonists and the slavers, then anyone with a bit of disposable income and a desire to escape the malarial mainland for a week or two. I didn't know any of that, of course, just that my mother visited with her parents and brothers in the 1960s, then again with my father on their honeymoon in 1980, and in April 1995 they returned again, this time accompanied by two children and one recent widow with an even more recently broken ankle. Nana's crutches rattled on the floorboard, my mother read aloud every billboard, and my father played the same three Nanci Griffith tapes over and over all the way down from Tennessee. When we arrived at our rental house on the island's marshy south end, we drove right up underneath. Beyond the wooden pilings, a million blue eyes of the ocean fluttered and winked. So innocent. But I had my doubts.

* * *

Sunday was Easter. Sarah and I ate jelly beans for breakfast then ran down the splintery front staircase to the beach. The water was tepid and foamy at the edges. I stopped where the sand was still dry but she ran ahead, her skinny white arms flying up to greet every wave that rolled in. I had this feeling—one I'd always had, maybe, but which was lately announcing itself with increasing petulance—that something bad was about to happen. Or that something bad had already happened and I just didn't know about it yet. That what seemed safe was actually dangerous, that what seemed permanent was in fact flimsy and false. When I was little, on a rerun of *Flipper*, I saw baby sharks swimming in the shallows. Now I thought about the baby sharks. I thought about the grownup sharks they must have become. I thought about the lionfish with its stinging frills and the angler fish's horrible underbite, the jellyfish and the giant squids and the electric eels sliding in and out of their terrible holes. They were all out there, and now so was my sister. I waded into the water just far enough that she technically wasn't alone. When a low wave surged in, my feet disappeared. When the wave went back out, it sucked the sand out from under me in a greedy rush that made it look and feel like I was getting pulled backward by some invisible hands. When I looked up, dizzy, I saw I was standing right where I'd always been.

Nana hobbled down the stairs and staked her crutches into the sand. Under her bandages, her ankle was fat and purple and green. Weeks earlier, she'd tripped and fallen in the hall at Pigeon Roost. Alone in the big house, she had to crawl to the telephone to call her sister. When anyone asked what she fell over, she shrugged and said, "Invisible bump." Now she wore dark sunglasses and stared out at the ocean, shifting her weight from crutch to crutch, sinking into the sand as the tide washed in and out around her. I stood and stared with her. I was watching out for my sister and also for dolphins, the one good thing that lived in the ocean. I kept thinking I saw them but always my eyes were tricking me.

* * *

Monday we went to the general store and I bought a pink foam boogie board and a postcard of a ghost. He stood on a dune in a wide-brimmed hat, one arm raised toward the ocean, his body half-disappeared into the overcast sky. This was the Gray Man, a wisp of a legend for a wisp of an island. Some people said he was the ghost of a colonist who drowned in the marsh. Others said he was the ghost of Blackbeard the Pirate, whose ships had trawled the coast nearby. But everyone agreed he appeared only in the hours before a hurricane, and that anyone who saw him was spared from the storm's destruction. It was months away from hurricane season but for the rest of the week I kept an eye out just in case. Not seeing him was always a relief. But I knew it didn't mean nothing bad was coming, only that I wouldn't be spared if it did.

* * *

Tuesday I took the boogie board down to the water. I waded out far enough that I could float but still see the sandy bottom. A little wave came along and I let it shuttle me back to shore, then I pushed myself out again. I did this for a while, in and out, in and out. Every time I scudded back onto the sand, I pushed myself further and further back into the water. It wasn't so bad, after all. I was maybe even prac-tically surfing. Then, one trip beachward, as the board and my body behind it dragged against the sand, I felt a mean pinch on the fat of my bare leg. The shock of it propelled me out of the water and into the air. I collapsed onto the sand and rolled over to examine my leg, sure I'd see the crab still dangling from my flesh, but all that remained were two purple-red dots, an inch apart on my upper thigh. My mother saw it all from up on the deck. In the bathroom, hydrogen peroxide fizzing on the minuscule wounds, she shook her head and laughed. "Girl, you walked on water." Everyone thought it was cool when Jesus did that, but I did not feel cool. That was it for the week. I didn't go back into the ocean again.

* * *

Wednesday I shuffled out into the living room and found my parents and grandmother staring at the television. It was bolted up into the corner of the room, like in a hospital, and turned to the news. On the screen there was a big brown building, half on fire, half falling into a giant hole. There was a man with a microphone. There were grownups in business clothes, some of them bloody. There were fire-fighters and ambulances and a lot of people crying. I stood silent, staring at the screen, for a long time. When my mother turned and realized I was there, she jumped up and shooed me outside. I stayed out on the deck until my curiosity became unbearable and then I went back inside. I needed to eat breakfast, and then I needed to practice my Easter yo-yo, and then I needed to eat some Easter candy, needed to unwrap a Rolo very slowly, place it into my mouth very slowly, chew it very slowly, all while staring at the screen, until my mother shooed me outside again.

All day it was like that, back and forth. Inside: smoking building, hole in the street, a bloody fireman carrying a bloody, flopping child. Whenever they showed Oklahoma City on the map of the United States, the red dot appeared right in the middle, right in the gut. Outside, up and down the beach, kids rode lazy waves on their boogie boards, parents applied and reapplied sunscreen, old fishermen reeled in their empty lines and cast them out again. No one else seemed to know that anything was happening anywhere else. If I stayed out there long enough I could almost forget too. I sat on my boogie board in the sand. When I squinted hard at where the water met the sky, I thought I could see land, another country. I wondered what the crab who bit me was doing, or if it had been eaten by something like it tried to eat me. I'd given up on the dolphins. But then someone cried, "Look!" And there they were, slicing through the waves, black gashes through the blue.

* * *

Thursday my father drove us down an inland highway lined with piney woods and old women selling seagrass baskets from roadside shacks all the way into Charleston. The city looked like the set of an old movie but all the extras were in too-new clothes. The buildings leaned into one another, pale and chalky. The narrow streets were jammed with cars and, here and there, horse-drawn carriages. We followed one to a big red barn down a cobblestone alley near the port. My father bought five tickets.

Our driver wore a top hat and Nana's crutches stuck out the side of the buggy. We clomped around town. The palmettos tossed their fronds in the breeze and Spanish moss hung in globs from oak trees the driver said were older than the city itself. He gestured with his crop at the notable sites: a house occupied by the British army in one war and the Union army in another, the old city jail (obviously haunted), the white-steepled churches and their tight-packed graveyards (I looked away). He pointed out blocks rebuilt after earthquakes and hurricanes and facades that bore scars from Civil War artillery fire. He nodded down a side street toward something called The Old Slave Mart. "And that over there," he said as we idled at the next red light, "is the home of the CEO of Piggly Wiggly!" We all craned our necks to see the grand white portico and the bronze swine flanking the front stairs. Then the light turned green and the horses took us back to the barn.

My family left the city at sunset. By the time we were back on the highway, the world was dark again. My father put in another Nanci Griffith tape; my mother sighed. My sister and grandmother fell asleep and I tried to join them, but my head kept snapping forward and my seatbelt wanted to strangle me. Out the window wavered the distant shadows of tall, thin trees. When another car's headlights hit just right, my own face stared back at me. I felt sad and scared, a new kind of sad and scared, not the kind I'd been feeling for months now, since Grandaddy died, since Unk died. Something had got into me, crawled into me, an itch I couldn't find with my fingers. Part of me was back in Charleston, rolling through the city in the back of that buggy, looking up at the same old buildings little girls in buggies had been looking up at for two hundred years or more. Most of those girls were dead now—dead five, ten, twenty times longer than I'd been alive. They came and went but the buildings remained, the cobble-stone streets, the muggy breeze off the harbor. I knew I was going to cry, knew I'd lose if I fought it, knew that if anyone heard me and asked what was wrong I wouldn't know what to say. It wasn't all the ghosts of the old city or how we used to buy and sell people like horses or the war we fought because of it. It wasn't the building on the news or the hole in the street or the bloody children, or my grandfather and how he was dead, or my grandmother alone with no one to hear her fall. It wasn't the sharks or the eels or any other terrible thing in the ocean. It wasn't all the other kids who seemed to know how to be a kid better than me. It wasn't my sudden memory of our house back in Chattanooga, dark and empty and alone without us. It wasn't and it was, I didn't know, I couldn't say. Nanci Griffith was singing, "It's a hard life, it's a hard life, it's a very hard life, it's a hard life wherever you go," and I breathed in steady, let my nose run instead of snuffling all the snot back in. Was it really? Everywhere, all the same? I wasn't sure if that could be true but the waves of strange sadness rolled over me and I curled into them, glad for the darkness and my sleeping family, glad for my father with his eyes on the road. And the song ended and another began and we rolled through the night toward our temporary home, and the ocean in the dark, and everything else I couldn't yet see.

* * *

Friday, our last night at the beach, my mother boiled shrimp. When their gray bodies curled up and turned pink she drained the pot and dumped them into a big bowl of ice cubes in the middle of the table. My father showed me how to pinch off the soft fringe of legs, pry off the translucent shell, and pinch off the tail. We peeled and plunged our spoils into cocktail sauce until the pile of empty shells was larger than the pile of shrimp had ever been.

After dinner, I picked an apple from a bowl on the counter. I took one bite, chewed, swallowed, and then felt something go wrong. The flesh inside my cheeks and my tongue and even my teeth began to itch and soon my stomach was rolling over and over like it was caught inside a wave. I didn't know what was happening but I knew what was going to happen.

I didn't say anything, just walked to the bathroom, bent over the toilet, pulled back my hair, and puked. Then I rinsed my mouth and returned to the kitchen.

"I just threw up!" I announced to my family.

Everyone made their own personal noises of disgust. "Bless your heart!" Nana said. "I hope it wasn't one of those shrimps didn't agree with you."

"I think it was the apple," I said. My mother jumped up to feel my forehead and I pulled away. "It was the *apple*," I said again, but she picked up the bowl of shrimp shells from the table and, without a glance at her mother-in-law, dumped them in the trash.

Saturday we got back to Chattanooga and everything was greener than when we left. Our house had gone musty in our absence and everything felt creepy and too-quiet. The answering machine light blinked. When my father turned on the TV, everyone was talking about Oklahoma City. They were playing and replaying the same clips of the same smoking building and the same people running and the same bloody flopping child. I thought, *I am going to be seeing this for the rest of my life.*

Weeks later, I wandered into the kitchen and found my mother slicing an apple. "Want some?" she said, angling her knife through the red skin.

"Don't you remember what happened at the beach?" I said.

"I don't think that was the apple," she said. "It was probably a bad shrimp."

But I knew I was right, and I knew there was only one

way to make her understand. I took another apple from the bowl and took three big bites. I chewed with my mouth open, rudely, staring right at her. She stared back at me with one arched eyebrow. Soon enough, my mouth began to itch and the itch spread down my throat and my stomach began to churn. I walked to the bathroom and my mother followed. I puked it all up and then some and she said, "Well, honey!" But I was fine. Better than fine. It was a relief, for once, to feel so sure.

Prime Meridian

On what I once thought of as the horizon of my childhood, sixth grade shimmered like Shangri-La. No more bright colors and rounded edges, no more recess, no more kid stuff. There, in the beige halls of middle school, I would ascend to a higher plane: I would have a homeroom and a locker combination, I would have a weekly planner and midterms and finals, there would be Student Council elections and Friday night dances, there was even the strangely alluring requirement that I "dress out" for P.E. class, which suggested that I might be asked to do powerful new things with my body as well as my mind.

The locker room was gray and muggy and had a sharp, sour smell, and some girls said there were holes in the wall and the boys were peeking through at us, and I wondered if their B.O. was wafting through too, because surely *we* didn't stink so bad. I changed with frantic quickness out of my all-wrong jeans and baggy T-shirt and into my all-wrong Umbro knockoffs and bigger, baggier T-shirt, keeping my head down and my eyes unfocused—if I couldn't see myself, nobody else could see me either. I didn't hate my body, not the way some girls did, the ones who stood before the wide warped mirror over the sinks pinching their thighs and bellies and frowning at their own faces, running their palms down the bridges of their noses like they were moldable into other, better shapes. These girls were always rolling their gym shorts up by the waistbands and tugging their shirts back to look tighter, but I didn't mind, I liked looking like a boxy lump, a lumpy box. Hating my body would have required me to be familiar enough with its specifics to assess its flaws. I'd realized too late the best part of being a kid: the unremarkability of my physical being, the generic privacy of it. Once I'd grown without thinking of it as growing, just forever becoming a taller version of my previous self, and I would have been happy to continue scaling up to infinity if it meant keeping all my standard proportions and functions intact. But my body seemed set on betraying me in all the usual ways, all the invisible inside changes becoming unignorable outside changes, demanding deodorant and packs of pink razors and miserable trips with my mother to the Intimates department at Sears. A training bra? For what, exactly, did my boobs need to be trained? Would they grow in some wrong direction otherwise? And would that be worse to endure, really, than the constant Lycra chafe, the threat of a slipped-down strap, the plastic adjuster-thingies simultaneously gouging into my shoulder blades popping out to announce my bra-wearingness to the whole wide world?

Once we were dressed out, everyone shuffled into the gym, blinking under the buzzing fluorescents, girls to one side and boys to the other. We performed a few rounds of perfunctory calisthenics, and then we ran. Coach Pickens, with her feathered bangs and her stopwatch and her whistle, would yell, "Twenty minutes!" and it would begin, the slow pounding of thirty-something pairs of sneakers, Adidas and Sketchers and my own Walmart whatevers, around and around the gym in a great greasy circle. I kept pace with my friend Cindy. We narrated our misery between ragged breaths. "You know," she panted one day, lowering her voice and narrowing her eyes as we passed Coach Pickens, "in the state of Tennessee, murder is a capital offense." Cindy and I sat next to each other in homeroom for a while but didn't become friends until the day she leaned over and told me about the time she slammed her finger in a car door then developed gangrene so doctors had to do an experimental surgery to replace it with a lifelike prosthetic. "That's why I can do *this*," she'd said, bending the tip of her pointer finger back so far her fingernail almost touched her second knuckle. She had a twin sister and a pet husky and she liked Jesus and read big fat Stephen King novels. I thought she was so great I didn't even mind a few weeks later when she confessed that she'd been lying about her finger, she was just double-jointed.

Twenty minutes! What was it? A formless thing of expanding, shifting weight we seemed to be responsible for moving with our own bodies. If we did not move forward, time did not either. Coach Pickens stood there with her whistle dangling from her bottom lip like a cigarette. "Get a move on, ladies!" she would bellow every now and then, which served as a general prod and included the boys in the class but in particular was directed at a pack of girls—the local originators of the rolled waistbands, the most active locker room mirror-frowners—who as always were running so slowly they threatened to topple over with each step. "But we're on our *periods*!" the girls would yell back together, and Coach Pickens would soften, and nod, and wave away her own demand. The first time it happened, I was aghast. When I was running, there was almost nothing in the world I wanted more than to stop running, but even I couldn't imagine the level of desperation that might drive you to admit that you'd started your period, let alone that you were actively on it right that moment, and not just admitting it but yelling it out for your whole co-ed P.E. class to hear. It didn't occur to me that these girls might be lying until the day Cindy said, "Man, they've been on their periods for like half the semester. Gotta be getting anemic by now."

When Coach Pickens finally blew the whistle, it always came out like a long, sad scream. Our sneakers screeched to a stop and we moved along to dodgeball, or kickball, or whatever else had been set as the day's next indignity.

* * *

It was less difficult than it had once been to project myself into the future, to believe that one day I might become something like an adult, but it was still not exactly easy. One afternoon, not long after my age reached double-digits, my mother had appeared in my bedroom doorway holding a book, which she handed to me with such effortful casualness that I was suspicious before I even read the name, which was *What's Happening to Me?* "I thought you might want to read this," she said. I'd shoved the book between my mattress and box-spring before she was halfway back downstairs. I let it live there for the next several years, pulling it out only whenever the question of the title weighed especially heavy on my mind, and always surreptitiously, like it was hardcore pornography and not a guide to puberty first published in the 1970s and illustrated accordingly.

On one page, a classroom of funky cartoon children were shown staring at a chart, more realistically drawn, of a naked female body progressing from eight to eighteen years old. The girl at "11 to 12 years old" looked enough like me at the time that I took the renderings of her future bodies as

52

projections of my own. But I was skeptical. I considered with dread the "17 to 18 years old" version of myself, with her wide hips and narrow waist, her high, round boobs, the tidy dark triangle of her crotch. The book said, at that point, though my emotional development would continue, my physical development would be complete, which suggested to me that I would inhabit that particular version of my body for the rest of my life, from age 18 until whenever I would die, and it seemed like the kind of body I was supposed to want to have, but the idea of it pained me; I felt an imaginary belt cinching around my waist, two hard orbs forcing themselves out of my ribcage. If the chart had been a menu of future options, I would have chosen the "13 to 14 years old" model. I would take one step up from my current self then stay right there forever. That seemed like more than enough.

But even then I sensed that this "complete" 18-year-old body couldn't truly be an endpoint. None of the women I knew looked like clothed versions of that naked girl, and none of the men looked like clothed versions of the naked boy on the opposite page. Maybe they once had, but some force greater than puberty had picked them up and hauled them into middle age, further stretching and crinkling and widening and sharpening. I knew kids my age, and I knew my parents and grandparents and aunts and uncles and teachers, but in between were twenty or thirty years that I couldn't account for. Whatever was happening to me, I was over it. But these people who were not kids anymore but not quite adults—what was happening to *them*?

On the first day of seventh grade, I was unexpectedly offered a view into this shadowy gap. My third-period Geography class was supposed to be taught by a fifty-something man named Coach Sneed. The classroom, when I walked in, looked as it must have for years: bulletin boards covered with sun-faded world maps, tall filing cabinets plastered with snapshots of his wrestlers at wrestling matches, a wide metal desk cluttered with framed photos of his two extremely fat chihuahuas, including several of him holding one dog under each arm. Coach Sneed was a tall man with a cascading belly and a bristly black mustache; I'd heard he taught all of his classes while seated behind his desk, but the rolling chair was empty. Instead, a petite young woman stood by the chalkboard at the front of the room. She had the haircut I understood I was supposed to have but didn't, which I resented because it was called The Rachel. She was twisting a large diamond ring on her left hand. When the bell rang, the woman cleared her throat and smiled a big white smile. "Hi, y'all!" she said, and waved like she was trying to catch someone's eye across the cafeteria.

"Are you Coach Sneed?" asked someone who knew perfectly well that she wasn't Coach Sneed.

"No, I'm Miss Paulson," the woman said, very seriously. "Coach Sneed is so sorry he couldn't be with y'all on your first day. He's out sick, but he'll be back in no time, okay? In the meantime, I'll be your substitute. He left y'all some worksheets—"

A boy raised his hand. Miss Paulson pointed at him. "How old are you?" he asked.

She blinked. "I'm twenty-three."

Twenty-three! I thought, abruptly intrigued. I couldn't remember ever meeting someone who was twenty-three.

"Are you in college?" a girl asked.

College!

"No, I graduated this past spring."

Graduated!

Another boy raised his hand but didn't wait for her to point before he said, "Are you, like, single?"

"I am not," Miss Paulson said, barely suppressing her grin.

"Boo," said the boy.

"In fact," she continued, "I just got engaged! I'm getting married in a few months. But Coach Sneed will be back by then and I'll be long gone." She tried again to hand out the worksheets, but now the questions only multiplied. How did her fiancé propose? Where were they getting married? How many bridesmaids would she have? What about her dress? (I had questions of my own, but was too in awe to speak: Did she have her own apartment? Did she have AOL? Did she have a Pier One papasan chair? Did she look the way she thought she'd look when she was thirteen? Did she feel the way she thought she would feel?) She seemed unable or unwilling to resist the barrage until someone asked, "Do you want to be a Geography teacher, too?" and she grabbed on as if to a life preserver. "Well, I've always dreamed of teaching kindergarten," she said, "but what I really want is to start a family. I love babies. I want to have a *lot* of babies."

A gaggle of girls squealed. I slumped, deflated. This was not the twenty-three-year-old for me.

That night, I got a phone call from my friend Jessie. "Did you hear about Coach Sneed?" she asked. I hadn't, I said. "Well, a girl in my neighborhood's mom works at the hospital and she just called to tell me her mom just came home to tell her that he's *dead*." This was the first time—and would turn out to be the last time—anyone ever called me specifically to deliver gossip. "It's probably just a rumor," my own mother said when I hung up and ran downstairs with the news, and I decided to believe her, but at school the next morning all the teachers had red eyes and red noses, their second-day smiles thin and forced. A heart attack, someone said. "I'm so sorry," the teachers kept saying to us. "He was such a wonderful man. I'm so sorry," over and over again, as if we'd lost our favorite uncle and not a Geography teacher we'd never met.

Then again, Miss Paulson had never met him, either, and she looked saddest of all. In third period, her big white smile was bigger and whiter than the day before, and the more she forced it—that day, and the next, and in the days and weeks that followed, as her temporary tenure stretched on and on—the more her teeth came to look like two rows of menacing Chiclets, and never more so than the morning in October when she announced to us Coach Sneed's permanent replacement: "It's me!"

We arrived the following Monday to find the classroom redecorated. Gone were the wrestlers and chihuahuas, gone were the faded maps. Now the bulletin board asked, in bubbly cut-out letters, "WHERE ARE WE?" Underneath was a crisp map of Tennessee. As if anyone could possibly forget. As if the rest of the world did not exist, or was simply irrelevant. Most class periods resembled the first one, with her valiantly attempting to distribute various worksheets and my classmates hounding her with questions and wild stabs at flirtation that she increasingly seemed to resent but developed no reliable defense mechanism against. Sometimes I forgot what had actually happened and found myself praying, feebly: *Dear God, please let Coach Sneed come back soon.* I never knew him so I couldn't miss him, exactly; I just wanted what I once thought I was supposed to have. Sometimes I caught a glimpse of Miss Paulson across the chaos of the classroom that was now hers and I wondered if she felt the same.

* * *

I knew, because I was told, that kids of a certain age always think of themselves as invincible. I enjoyed fancying myself an exception to this rule, but I must have known even then that it wasn't a rule, not anything so absolute, because I also sensed that a keen awareness of vulnerability was largely indivisible from the whole teenaged enterprise. We were all individual accumulations of weak spots, some more aware of it than others, some more keen to protect themselves than others, some more desperate than keen. The best-case scenario was something like mutually assured destruction, but even that required a vigilance beyond most of our capacities. Early in the fall of seventh grade, the county health department held a vaccination clinic in my school's cafeteria: boosters of childhood shots, first doses against Hepatitis B and meningitis, chicken pox for anyone who'd escaped childhood without it (not me, and I had the scars to prove it). The only kids I remember crying were boys, their faces crumpling like pink paper. The next day, in Geography, one of them, a football player, bragged loudly about how he'd flexed his bicep the second the nurse stuck the needle in. "Blood went *everywhere!*" he crowed, and then another boy frogged him hard in the arm, right in the tender meat, and he howled and doubled over and everyone laughed.

My school was set far back off a two-lane highway, a wide parking lot and a muddy field away from a dispatch garage for the county's emergency services, and it wasn't unusual throughout the day to hear ambulance sirens start up and go wailing out into the world, brief bursts of urgency always directed elsewhere. One morning in November, sitting in the auditorium with my first-period class—an interdisciplinary seminar offered to students pegged as gifted, as if in recompense for the rest of the middle-school experience, and taught by a sweet, perpetually frazzled woman named Mrs. Frye—I heard the strange sound of sirens not fading away but growing closer, then closer and closer. When someone opened the double-doors to the lobby, we could see through the front windows that the front curb was lined with ambulances and fire trucks, silent now, lights flashing. Past the front office, on the landing, an empty stretcher sat unattended. "Maybe somebody *died*," I whispered to Cindy, who said, "Oooh," and rolled her eyes. We giggled our way up the stairs to the cafeteria, then stopped. It was barely nine o'clock, but some of the fold-up lunch tables were already folded down and packed with other seventh graders, all of them dressed out for P.E. class. Their faces were red, like they'd just been running, but also strange and blank. Some were talking in low voices but most sat quiet, a wholly unnatural state.

Mrs. Frye shooed us back to our classroom and followed a few minutes later with the news she knew we all craved. "It seems that a boy collapsed while running in gym," she said. "A seventh grader—Tyler Nickelman? Do any of you know him?" A clamor erupted. We all knew him. Most of us had been in school with him since kindergarten. He was one of those kids who still, actually, looked mostly like he had in kindergarten: glasses, bowl cut, kind of chubby. He lived in a subdivision over the hill from mine and rode my bus, and he'd gone out with my friend Beth-Anne, who also rode our bus, before she moved to Nashville the summer before. "Oh, I'm sure he'll be fine," Mrs. Frye said, waving away the tizzy she'd brewed among us. "I think the ambulance was just a precaution." *Precaution.* I rolled the word around in my mouth like a Life Saver until it dissolved.

In the hall between classes, I saw kids who looked like they'd been crying, boys mostly, some boys who I knew were friends with Tyler, others who I'd never realized had friends at all. Teachers stood in their classroom doorways, looking over and through us to exchange looks with one another, lips tight, arms crossed across their sweaters. In Geography, Miss Paulson's smile was wide and bright, nervous and unnerving. When the intercom crackled on, the principal apologizing for the interruption but he had some sad news to share, she said, "Quiet now, y'all," but for once we already were.

On the bus that afternoon, when we came to Tyler's stop, I watched the driver look up and scan his wide rearview mirror to see if the boy was scrambling down the aisle like usual. He idled there for a few seconds before some kid yelled, "He's not coming. He's dead!" The driver shrugged and then rumbled us on down the road. I wondered when he would realize it hadn't been a joke.

It's a wonder to me, even now, how you can know that something is possible—inevitable, even—and still be surprised when it happens. I knew about death. I had known about it for so long. I knew that adults died, and I knew that kids died sometimes too. But now it had really happened. And to Tyler Nickelman, of all people. Six months earlier, I'd watched him and Beth-Anne slow-dancing at the Spring Fling just before she moved away: arms out straight, hands on each others' shoulders, party lights reflecting off their glasses so I couldn't see their eyes but they were both smiling. From my perch up in the bleachers, I'd thought, *Those two? Dancing?* Now I thought, *That kid? Dead?*

The next day, all the teachers seemed to have been made to memorize the same speech about what happened: "Yesterday, as you may know, one of your classmates collapsed while running laps in the gym. An ambulance came and took him to the hospital, but he didn't make it. If you want to talk to a guidance counselor, Mrs. Singer's door is always open." Poor them. Poor Mrs. Singer. Poor Coach

Pickens, who—it took me years to realize—must have been standing there with her whistle in her mouth when it happened. Nobody knew quite what to do. Wild speculation took root in my classmates' collective incomprehension. "Is it true?" a boy asked Miss Paulson in third period. "No one has to run laps in P.E. anymore because Tyler Nickelman died?"

"I heard they were *cancelling* P.E.," someone else said.

"It's only right," a girl said. "Like, I mean, *he died.*"

Miss Paulson shook her head. "I know y'all are upset," she said in her sweetest kindergarten voice. "But Tyler didn't die because he was running laps. The timing was just a terrible coincidence. The doctors say he had a heart defect, something he was born with. He could've just as easily died bending down to tie his shoes." Her smile looked like a real one now, not forced; she seemed pleased to be offering what she thought of as comforting truth. "So you see," she said, "it's nothing to worry about!" And out came the worksheets again.

* * *

Seventh grade in general, and Geography in particular, I often felt as if I wasn't learning anything. But of course that wasn't true. I learned, for instance, that Tennessee has 95 counties, and the difference between an archipelago and a peninsula, and at least two new circumstances in which I might die. I learned that even when something shimmers on the horizon, when it comes closer, the shimmer doesn't always come with it. I learned that the future is temporary, and the present too, and not even the past is static. I didn't have to run or walk or push my way through anything to make time pass; it just did. It would never stop. And even when it did, for me, it would go on for everyone else.

60

Tyler died and then it was Thanksgiving, then Christmas, New Years, Valentine's Day. We kept running in P.E. class. We had another vaccine clinic and the boys cried again. Miss Paulson got married and left us with a sub for a week, a substitute for a substitute, and came back as Mrs. Hanover. Everyone was trying to become somebody else, but she really did it, but she was just the same. In the spring we got our yearbooks and when I found my picture I felt strange to myself, familiar and alien all at once, the way I felt when I saw my own baby photos but this one was taken only a few months earlier. There was a full-page photo of Coach Sneed and a full-page photo of Tyler Nickelman; the yearbook was dedicated to them both, and I'd never thought about it before but now I saw that they looked enough alike—round faces, glasses, blunt-cut hair— that the photos might have been of the same person many years apart. "In memoriam," the yearbook said, and I would remember, but sometimes I would forget. In idle moments, in years to come, I would find myself wondering about him the way I wondered about so many other kids from middle school, the ones who transferred to private school or moved away or simply, one day, never showed up again—what became of him? How is he doing? My fingers would drift over to a search bar and sometimes I wouldn't remember what I wouldn't find until I'd already typed his name.

Wild Things

In eighth grade, I shared a bus stop with a bunch of high school boys. They ignored me completely and I pretended to return the favor, but in the 6:45 a.m. quiet, it was impossible not to hear every word they said. "Oh my God, man, I'm like, so tired man," one would say, and another would say, "I know, right? My mom kept banging on my door this morning like, 'Get up dumbass, you're gonna miss the bus and I'm not driving you this time,' and I was like, I wish I'd miss that fuckin' bus, then I could just fuckin' hang out here and play *Madden*." They cursed with remarkable fluency, I'd never heard anything like it. Some mornings, one boy would produce a purple Crown Royal bag, like the one Marie used to keep her Barbie shoes in. "Hell yeah," the others would say, and a minute later I'd hear the snick-snick of a lighter and a series of long inhales and exhales before they started talking again. "Y'all hear Derek's mom found his stash?" "Yeah, he's grounded until, like, college." "You dumbass, that dumbass ain't going to college." When their smoke wafted my way, I coughed and they snickered. That was the only time I knew they knew I was there. I waited for them to offer me a drag. My class had done D.A.R.E. in fifth grade and I still remembered all the ways to just say no; I planned to deploy "the cold shoulder." I waited and waited. I'd been waiting for years, I was so ready. But the bus always came before they could ask.

* * *

That year, 1998 falling into 1999, I took a class called Junior Latin. It was called Junior Latin despite the fact that there was no Senior Latin to ascend to, at least not at the high school my middle school fed into, at least not anymore. The burden of the whole dead language fell upon the shoulders of one Mrs. Molina. She was a round woman with a round face and round brown curls and on day one she pumped her round fists in the air to emphasize our first and most enduring lesson: "Sex rules!" It was an imprecise but effective mnemonic for recalling grammatical gender and also the unofficial tagline of the course. I still can't believe what she got away with; perhaps the school had forgotten that she—and the class, if not Latin itself—even existed. Her true passion was mythology, an imprecise mix of Roman and Greek, and she relayed all stories of the gods and goddesses like it was the juiciest, freshest gossip. Had we heard about Zeus turning himself into a white bull to seduce those mortal women? What about his daughter Persephone, bless her heart, lured into the underworld by that good-for-nothing Hades? Hera was always fuming over some perceived slight, Cupid and Aphrodite always plotting someone's demise, and Hercules—well, we watched a lot of movies about Hercules. "Look at those *thighs*!" Mrs. Molina would say, making grabby hands at the screen of the TV, even at the Disney cartoon.

The gods and goddesses were absolutely unlike us in every single way. They were unkillable, untethered, free to roam Heaven and Earth, with every force of nature at their perfect fingertips. Their personalities were distinct and known to all, like the Spice Girls. And they were all having sex pretty much whenever and with whoever or whatever they wanted. All except Artemis, who I picked as my favorite. Daughter of Zeus and Leto, twin sister of Apollo, goddess of the hunt and the moon, protectress of the young, Lady of Wild Things, huntress-in-chief to the gods. I knew her first as Diana, her name in the Greek pantheon, her name in art. There was a sculpture garden near Pawleys Island that my family liked to visit when we went on vacation, and on the previous spring break I'd noticed her there for the first time. She was everywhere I looked: balanced on a sphere, bow held high; running, caught forever midair; flanked by hounds and stags; draped in rippling tunics; naked as the day she was born. All the other stone girls carried vases or pressed themselves against stone men or cradled squirming stone children. But she only hunted. She made it look easy. I'd tried archery a few times at Girl Scout camp and no matter how hard I screwed up my face, my arrows always landed four feet shy of or ten feet beyond my hay-bale target. But her face was blank and perfect and her arrows landed wherever she wanted. She was solid and smooth and glowing in the sun; I was one hundred pounds of rocks in a girl-shaped sack. I had taken to swaddling myself daily in a red fleece pullover, trying to trick myself and the world into forgetting I had any sort of body at all. Artemis wasn't in many of the stories Mrs. Molina told, but I liked that too. She seemed immune to the tomfoolery that filled their endless days. She was down on earth tending to her creatures. She wasn't in the other gods' stories because she was in her own.

My favorite went like this: One day, she was bathing in a secret pool in the forest when a mortal man appeared.

He'd been out hunting with his friends when his hounds ran away. He was looking for them when he came across Artemis, and when he saw her he stopped and stared, totally stunned to be in the presence of a goddess. But when she saw him, she was *pissed*. How dare he disturb her secret goddess bath? How dare he stare at her secret goddess body? Her bow and arrows were out of reach or she'd have shot him straight away. Instead, she splashed him. The water was enchanted, and when it washed over him he turned into an elk. But only his body. His human mind remained. Artemis was pleased with herself and turned back to her bath. The man was terrified and ran away into the woods. He tried to call out for help but he couldn't speak. And then he found his hounds, the ones he'd been looking for. They'd been looking for him too, or for what he now appeared to be. They lunged at the elk and tore him to the ground.

* * *

For a week that year, my science class was usurped by a woman representing a local organization called WhyKnow, the logo of which, present on the many photocopied handouts she distributed, particularly emphasized the "n" and the "o," "no" being what we were supposed to say to having sex until we were married. The woman was pregnant, more pregnant than I'd ever realized a person could be—with a baby, I assumed, but also with wisdom she seemed desperate to impart. She told us that we couldn't get pregnant from a swimming pool, just like we couldn't get pregnant by hugging or kissing or shaking hands, possibilities I'd never considered but apparently somebody had. She told us, also, that condoms don't work, birth control pills don't work, the pull-out method (the *what?*) doesn't work, so the only reliable way we could avoid getting pregnant was to never have sex at all. "But babies are so cute, right?" she cooed at us one day. "Who thinks babies are *so cute*?" All the boys made gagging sounds and the girls raised their hands. I shivered in my red pullover. She called a lipgloss-addicted girl named Megan up to the front of the room then produced an unwieldy beige garment. She hefted it onto the girl and fastened a series of Velcro straps. Megan stumbled back under the new weight of her heavy, featureless boobs and heavy, featureless belly. I stared in horror at the two of them: the real pregnant woman and the fake pregnant girl and their symmetrical alien roundness. "Not so cute, huh?" the WhyKnow lady said, the only time all week I was sure she was speaking the truth, but Megan pursed her lips, unconvinced.

Another day, all the girls sat slumped against the lockers in the hall while the boys gagged and moaned inside the classroom, and then we traded places. I knew enough to know this was some kind of classic teenaged experience, but not enough to be prepared for what I saw on the slideshow, which lives in my mind still as a blur of swollen red flesh, angry white sores, lesions, pustules. And apparently I had something called a vulva? On Friday, the very pregnant woman passed around one final handout: the official WhyKnow pledge of abstinence. As my classmates and I read over the fine print, she stood at the front of the class-room rubbing her gigantic belly, smiling to herself like she knew a really good secret and wasn't telling anybody. I signed the pledge. I would have signed anything to make it stop.

That week had so little to do with what I thought of as my actual life, it might as well have been astronaut training. I did not have one smidgen of an ounce of a desire to become a mother, teen or otherwise, but even if I did, I figured I had a better chance of becoming the first girl to get pregnant from a swimming pool. I couldn't see how I would ever become a person who had sex. When I liked a boy, it was a momentous occasion to merely make eye contact with him; the prospect of exchanging casual physical touch was, quite literally, the stuff of my wildest dreams. At school we had a dance every quarter and I attended these faithfully, superstitiously almost, sitting with my friends in the bleachers, or sitting alone in the bleachers, pretending I wasn't watching all the boys I liked dancing with girl after girl who wasn't me, swaying to "Strawberry Wine" and that Boyz II Men song and that other Boyz II Men song. How did they do it? Sometimes I got brave, or bored, and went down into the crowd, nudging my body through the bodies like I was looking for someone, the way I used to wander around at recess when I didn't know what else to do. On a few occasions I felt a tap on my shoulder. Each time I turned around fast, hoping it was—oh, but it never was. Each time, the boy who wasn't the right boy said, "Hey, you wanna...?" and gestured vaguely at the swaying bodies all around us. If I'd been Artemis, I might have turned him into an elk. But I was myself, so I just turned around and ran.

* * *

Among the most alluring tales Mrs. Molina told that year were those of the Tennessee Junior Classical League's annual Latin Convention. Every April, schools across the state sent their brightest students to prove their mettle in various pseudo-Roman ways: written and oral exams, debate, drama, track and field. It went without saying that my public middle-school classmates and I would be trounced in all arenas by a bunch of private high-school kids. But the highlight, she assured us, was not a competition at all—it was the Saturday night dance, costumes required. "You could, of course, do a regular old bedsheet toga," she said with a wink. "But I say, if you have the chance, why not be a god?"

And so that spring my mother bought a few yards of scratchy brown cotton and cut a pattern from the one dress in my closet that I didn't entirely hate. We took the pieces over to my grandparents' house to use Nannie's sewing machine. My grandmother's art room featured a wall of bookshelves housing such titles as *The Women Who Run With Wolves* and *Ain't Nobody's Business If You Do: The Absurdity of Consensual Crimes in Our Free Country*. When my grandmother learned who I was dressing up as, she gasped. "Have you seen my portrait of the many-boobed Diana?" A few years earlier, at age seventy, Nannie had enrolled in community college to earn her associate's degree in art history. We were all very proud of her. But in one of her studio classes, she had produced a pencil drawing that I could barely let myself think about, let alone look at directly. Now she led me down the hall to where it hung, framed, on the wall outside the bathroom next to her mixed-media homage to Leonard Peltier. The grotesque body bore a hundred breasts, some round and full, others sagging like empty socks. The face was winking. The face was her own face, which meant it was sort of my mother's, which meant it was sort of mine too. "The goddess is such a powerful figure," she said, closing her eyes and pressing her hands to her heart. "You're going to be *beautiful*."

Back home, I retreated to my bedroom to try on the dress. We'd hot-glued gold rick-rack trim around the neckline and along the hem, which came up shorter than I expected, the cheap cotton rasping against my thigh. When I emerged, my mother placed a garland of fake autumn leaves on my head, then stepped back. "Well, don't you look *beautiful,*" she said, sounding almost surprised. I turned and studied myself in the mirror. I was surprised, too. I did look kind of beautiful. More than that, for the first time in a long time, maybe the first time ever, I looked exactly like I thought I should.

This fed a funny light feeling in me that only expanded as the weekend of Latin Convention grew closer. I had no great hopes for my performance on the state exam; long ago, I'd accepted that my Latin would remain forever Junior, the vocabulary and declension rules I'd memorized approximately as applicable to my life as the teachings of the WhyKnow woman. And so I temporarily replaced my academic ambition with a romantic one: I was going to go to Latin Convention and I was going to fall in love.

It would start in the host school's gymnasium at the opening ceremony. I'd catch the eye of some boy—a new boy, not one I'd been going to school with since we were snaggle-toothed illiterates. Maybe even a high-school boy. First I'd see him across the bleachers. Then, what luck, we'd be seated next to one another for the exam. He'd drop his number-two pencil and it would roll under my desk. I'd hand it back, but only after pretending like I wouldn't. That night, at the dance, he'd see me in my Artemis costume. He would be intimidated, because he would know his mythology, but he would introduce himself anyway. We would stand there making fun of everyone dancing, and then a slow song would come on, probably "I Don't Want To Miss A Thing"—I hated that song, hated Steven Tyler's scalded-cat yowling as much as I hated the idea of an asteroid destroying the planet before I could fall in love—but then the boy, this mysterious perfect boy, would say, "Hey, you wanna...?" And I wouldn't punish him, like Artemis. And I wouldn't run away, like myself. I would decide that nothing could hurt me. I would decide that something good might happen. For weeks I held onto this. Sometimes I lay awake at night thinking, *He's out there*. He was just a generic blur in my mind, blonde hair and braces, or brown hair and crooked teeth, but he was so real to me already. I couldn't wait to meet him. I couldn't wait to finally just say yes.

* * *

The second to last Tuesday that April, thirteen hundred miles away, two boys walked into their high school and killed twelve of their classmates and one of their teachers and then themselves. It wasn't the first time something like this happened. In the three years I'd been in middle school, there had been more and more until now there was a new one every few months: a new boy, a new town, a new gun. There was the boy with the twelve-gauge shotgun in Bethel, Alaska, and the boy with the pistol in West Paducah, Kentucky, and the boy with the rifle in Pearl, Mississippi. But the boys in Littleton, Colorado, had too many guns to remember. That afternoon, when I got off the bus, my mother was sitting on the couch watching CNN. I sat down next to her. When my sister got off the elementary school bus an hour later, she joined us. When my father got home from work, we ate dinner with the TV on—a sure sign of crisis in our household. It got dark in Tennessee, then dark in Colorado. The same footage looped all night. The same kids ran out the side door up the grassy hill with their hands on their heads. The same kids cried in their parents' arms in the parking lot. The boys' class photos kept flashing onto the screen: greasy hair, blank eyes. I'd never seen them before but they looked so familiar. In the morning, at the bus stop, I listened to the high school boys talking and smoking and I wondered if they had it in them, whatever "it" was. I wasn't sure they didn't.

On the bus to Latin Convention that Saturday, packed in with my fellow *discipuli* on the way from Chattanooga to Nashville, I remembered for the first time in days my previous plan for the weekend: my hopes of romantic conquest, or at least a slow dance. They seemed ridiculous now. How had I convinced myself this trip would be different from the whole rest of my life? Why did I think I was suddenly going to become this other version of myself, composed and fearless and desired? I hadn't even packed my red pullover. I had nowhere to hide. I was simmering in shame by the time we reached the host school, and as the bus parked among all the other buses, my waves of self-recrimination crested into dread. I'd never seen this school before but it was somehow familiar to me. I had a terrible feeling, not just a premonition of academic and romantic disappointment, and as I followed my classmates inside, herded by a bouncing Mrs. Molina from the bus to the crowded gymnasium, I began to understand why: This school looked to me just like the one that had been all over CNN all week. I was wrong; years later, two brief Google searches would set me straight. The high school in Littleton was a single-story, gray brick building with a wide front courtyard dotted with evergreen trees. The high school outside Nashville was a two-story, red brick building with a long breezeway entrance flanked by Bradford pears. I have no idea what mixed them up in my mind. But for the rest of that weekend I moved through one like I was moving through the other, as if what happened might at any moment start happening again. I'd expected to spend the whole time looking around for the boy who might love me, but now I was looking around for the one who might kill me. Were either of them here? How was I supposed to know? How was I supposed to tell the difference?

Nobody killed me during the opening ceremony, and

nobody killed me in the musty basement classroom where I bluffed my way through the state exam. Nobody killed me at the dramatic oratory competition or the debate or the relay race. Nobody fell in love with me either, so far as I could tell. But of course there was still the dance.

My classmates and I rode the bus to our hotel, changed out of our track pants and stovepipe jeans and into our togas, and rode the bus back to the school. We followed the throb of music through the dark halls back to the gym. The doors were flanked by fake marble columns and swags of silk ivy. A strange, loud song was playing; I couldn't tell what it was, I couldn't even see the DJ. A disco ball turned above a dance floor packed tight with self-styled Mt. Olympians, everyone bouncing up and down, togas slipping, crowns askew. A gym full of Tennessee teenagers pretending to be ancient immortals. Did they get the joke? Did they know it was a joke? Did they know how fragile they were?

When the song ended, everyone in the gym clapped and cheered and I realized it wasn't a DJ playing, it was a live band. The crowd shifted and I caught a glimpse of them, high school boys, the lead singer with a wild head of green hair. There would be no "Strawberry Wine," no Boyz II Men, no Aerosmith, thank god. There would be nothing like I wanted, nothing like I feared. The drummer tapped out the beat to the next song and the green-haired guy stepped up to the mic. When he began to sing, everyone around me threw their arms into the air and started to dance again. I didn't know this song either. I didn't know what to do. I was beginning to understand that what I wanted wasn't going to happen, at least not tonight, and what I feared wasn't going to happen either. After that, what was left? I stood frozen on the dance floor, afraid to push forward, afraid to turn back. Green-haired guy seemed to be building up to something, and all at once, everyone who knew the words, which seemed to be everyone I didn't know, which at this point seemed to be everyone, all sang together: "Make a little birdhouse in your soul!" The words made as much sense to me as Latin itself, less and less all the time, but finally I took a breath, threw my arms into the air, and started dancing too.

Drills

My high school was a sprawling, confounding structure, a two-story cylinder built in the seventies to which various wings and annexes had been appended every few years to keep up with the once-rural zone's long slide into suburbia. Everybody knew somebody who heard from someone that the people who built the school used the same blueprints they used to build prisons, and that felt true enough to me. The whole property—school, gym, tennis courts, softball field, baseball field, football field, other football field, parking lots filling all the gaps in between—was surrounded by a ten-foot chain-link fence edged along the top with barbed wire. There was a dairy farm across the road, a fact we were reminded of by every stiff southward breeze, and I figured the fence was to keep out the cows, until the day my friend Cindy said, "Ever noticed how the barbed wire is pointing *inwards?* That means *we're* the threat." And that felt true, too. The cows, of course, had a fence of their own.

The summer before ninth grade had run particularly thick with gossip, the kind that spread not just between kids but through parents too, which made it somehow more and less believable. In August, people said, the school would have metal detectors at every door, and armed guards would pat us down in the morning and patrol the hallways between classes, and we would have to carry see-through backpacks so we couldn't hide our guns inside. I found the backpack rumor especially chilling—some days, being in possession of a monogrammed L.L. Bean Deluxe felt like the only thing I was doing right—so of course that was the one my mother latched onto. When she saw see-through backpacks on sale at Walmart, she bought me a yellow one, the color of neon pee. "Just in case," she said, but I could tell she hated it too.

In the end, all we got was a new dress code. In the name of our own safety, my classmates and I were permitted to wear four colors of polo shirts: red, white, navy, and gray. We could wear two colors of pants: navy and khaki. We had to tuck our shirts into our pants and wear a belt: black or brown. No patch pockets, no logos bigger than a quarter, no patterned socks, no open-toed shoes, no hats, no hoodies, no jackets. In August, on the first day of school, we filled the gym for freshman orienta-tion, all three hundred-something of us wearing one of eight possible outfit combinations. The school principal, a tall, jowly man, stood at the podium. He welcomed us, the class of 2003, and thanked us for our compliance with the new precautions. "Now, you see," he said, "it will be easier for us to spot the troublemakers." Behind him, four vice principals sat in a row of white plastic lawn chairs, scan-ning the crowd with narrowed eyes. Troublemakers? I thought about Eddie Haskell. I thought about whoopee cushions and slingshots. I thought about the kid who might yearn with all his heart to bring a rifle to class but felt stymied by the ban on trench coats. I wasn't sure he existed. But I also wasn't sure I felt any safer, only more likely to die while wearing the same outfit as half of my classmates.

By then, well before then, what happened in Colorado had become known as Columbine, just Columbine. The name was the only thing anyone could agree on, unlike, for instance, whose fault it was. It was too simple, apparently, to blame the boys who did it, or the adults who helped them get the weapons they used. It had to be something else: the girls who rejected them, or the bullies who tormented them, or the video games they played, or *The Basketball Diaries* or *The Matrix*, or Marilyn Manson or Satan or Bill Clinton. Everyone was right and everyone else was wrong and if we didn't know who to blame then we didn't know who to punish, and if we didn't know who to punish then we didn't know how to keep it from happening again. We were all at the mercy of this apparently unsolvable mystery.

And so every morning I woke up and tucked my polo shirt into my khakis like a good little golf pro. I rode the bus. I went to class. I did my homework. Some days I stayed late for drama club or Model UN or Mock Trial. I tended my crushes like prized roses. I grew out my bangs. I turned fifteen. We had picture day. We got our pictures back from picture day. I didn't hate mine and I wondered if it was the one they'd show on the news with all the others. I'd got braces the spring before; I wondered if I'd still have braces when I died. I'd never held a gun in my life. I'd never even seen one up close outside a museum display case or a cop's hip holster. I didn't know enough to match their names with the things themselves. But I knew where I lived: It was Chattanooga, it was Tennessee, it was the United States of America. It was the Confederate flag buckle of the Bible Belt. It was Dixie Outfitters T-shirts under regulation polos. It was pickup trucks with gun racks and Browning Buckmark decals on the rear windshield. Even my father, who swerved his own pickup to avoid flattening squirrels, had a rusty old handgun of Grandaddy's in a crumbling cardboard box up in his bedroom closet. Every day I rode the bus and walked the halls and sat in class with boys who I knew had easy access to the means required to kill as many of us as they wanted. Girls too, but nobody worried about us.

I tended to favor the theory that it was other kids who'd driven the boys to it. I'd seen every day for years how cruel we could be. I wanted to think of myself as nice, but I knew I was mean too. "He's *weird*," I might say about a boy, and Cindy would say, "Yeah, but is he, like, *shoot-up-the-school* weird?" Then we would laugh, proving my point. In some idle moments I would try to catalog everything I might have done wrong—every snicker, every rolled eye, every carelessly cruel blow I might have dealt—trying to summon the face of anybody who might be, at that same moment, adding me to his list of names. Because these boys always had lists of names. Sometimes I thought about the boys I'd turned down at dances in middle school. I couldn't remember their names, only the looks on their faces before I turned and ran away. Sometimes I forgot about them completely. Sometimes when I made my list I came up empty. This was a relief, and no relief at all. Either I was safe or I would never see it coming.

* * *

Among so much else, I resented the danger for its late-breaking arrival. It's not that I thought my classmates and I were invincible; it's that I thought we'd covered the full gamut of relevant threats to our lives and how to protect ourselves against them way back in elementary school. There we had learned to buckle up, look both ways, never talk to strangers, and share everything but needles. There we learned, every October during Fire Prevention Week, how to sleep with our doors closed and crawl under the smoke and flee our burning houses via pre-planned evacuation routes. At school, when the bell rang for the fire drill, we learned to follow our teachers outside across the parking lot to the Dumpsters; and when the bell rang for the tornado drill, we learned to follow our teachers out into the hallway, kneel against the wall with our arms over our heads, and stay curled there until the bell rang again to signal the nonexistent storm had passed. The day I came home and told my mother about the tornado drills, she'd said, "God, that sounds like duck-and-cover." So then she had to explain the Cold War to her seven-year-old: how, when she was a kid, everyone thought Russia was going to drop a bomb on America, how at her elementary school she learned how to hide from that bomb under her desk. One winter, she said, Papa spent several damp, cold weeks digging a bomb shelter under their house so they could hide there if the bomb came when they were all at home. When I asked if Russia ever dropped the bomb, she laughed a weird laugh. "Well, we wouldn't be here if they had," she said. "But your grandfather did get pneumonia, and after that the basement flooded whenever it rained."

In the spring of my ninth-grade year, I don't know what committee of county administrators in which poorly lit conference room came to this conclusion, but somebody somewhere decided that we couldn't just dress our way into safety after all. They seemed to believe, now, that we needed to think of a school shooting the same way we thought about fires or tornados, the way people once thought about that bomb: assume its inevitability and teach the children how to keep themselves alive.

Our teachers told us what we would do but not when

we would do it. To the extent that there was a purpose, that would have defeated it. Instead, on a random day in the middle of a random class period, the bell would ring. "Teachers and students, this is a safety drill," the principal would intone over the intercom in his soporific drawl. "*This* —is a safety drill." At this cue, we would all slide from our desks to the floor and crawl to whichever corner of the room was least visible from the classroom doorway. Our teacher would dash to the door, check the hall for any stragglers, lock the door and cover its inset window, shut the window blinds, then join us in the corner. Meanwhile, the principal and his squadron of vice principals would go up and down all the hallways, banging on doors and jiggling the knobs, demanding to be let inside. We were supposed to ignore them. We were supposed to be quiet. We were just supposed to wait. We would wait and wait. We would crouch or kneel or lean against the wall or each other. We would fart. We would snicker. We would shush and snicker some more. Our feet would go numb in our closed-toed shoes. And finally, after some indeterminate length of time, the bell would ring and the intercom would crackle on again. "This concludes today's safety drill," the principal would say. "Thank you, teachers and students." But he never sounded especially grateful, just tired. I was tired too.

My freshman classmates and I were the last to experience our particular high school without these drills. After that spring, we were subject to them a few times per semester for the next three years, until we graduated. They have since become standard, of course, all the way down to kindergarten. It is strange to remember them as the new things they once were. After the second or third one they almost felt ordinary enough, like crouching against the wall in the hallway, like lining up by the Dumpsters. I wanted to believe it was better than nothing. I wanted to trust all the adults whose job it was to keep us safe. But I had questions, ones I felt I shouldn't ask, ones I had a feeling nobody could answer even if I did. Like, if this potential shooter we were hiding from was one of our own—which all previous incidents indicated he would be, just like all previous incidents indicated that he would be a he—then wouldn't he know what we learned doing the safety drills? If he was truly determined to kill a bunch of people, wouldn't he just find some way to work around all these flimsy precautions? Wouldn't he exploit one of the many scenarios we were never asked to plan for, like a shooter in the overcrowded halls between classes, a shooter in the overcrowded cafeteria during lunch, a shooter during one of the mandatory pep rallies that regularly superseded our afternoon classes during football and basketball and baseball season? Or what about during a fire drill, when all twelve hundred of us were lined up outside, or during a tornado drill, when we were all hunkered down in the hallways? Or what about during a safety drill itself? It was too perfect. It would be so easy. All of us already corralled and cowering. All of us trying to believe that a wooden door, when locked, became magically bulletproof. All of us assuming he wouldn't already be in the room.

I thought about it all the time, the inevitable failure of this plan. I thought about it without realizing I was thinking about it. It just became a habit of my teenage mind. I imagined my friends and classmates and teachers running, crying, bleeding. I imagined looking up at the boy with the gun in his hand and recognizing his face. I imagined knowing his mother's name, what bus he rode, what he'd looked like in first grade. Sometimes I tried to imagine being him. What would it be like to walk those confounding hallways, up and down and around and around, blasting away anyone in my path? What would it be like to be soaked with blood and not even know whose it was? What would it be like to be so full of whatever you needed to be full of for your life to take that turn? I didn't like thinking about it. I just wanted to make sure the idea didn't appeal to me. It didn't. Other times I tried to imagine what it would be like to get shot and die. The explosion of pain, the rearrangement, the dark slide into nothingness. Or I tried to imagine what it would be like to get shot and live. I read somewhere that it felt like getting pinched really hard or stung by a large bee. I'd felt some version of both sensations before. I told myself maybe it wouldn't be so bad—forgetting all the tears I'd cried over stubbed toes, all my good moods utterly derailed by a paper cut. If it had to happen, I hoped I would be in a classroom with a table. This wasn't part of the safety drill protocol but I heard about kids hiding under tables in the library at Columbine. Some of them died anyway, but not all of them. I didn't love the odds, but I did like having a plan of my own.

* * *

Years later, I would do the math: Between August 1999 and May 2003, the forty-six months that comprised my time in high school, there were twenty-three school shootings across the United States. I was surprised by the number; I thought it would be more. It was still too many. Sometimes it had felt like waiting to be picked for dodgeball—one by one, the chances going up every time it happened somewhere else. Even if you were dead last, you were bound to make the team. But, in the end: nothing. Once, during exams, some-body called in a bomb threat and we all had to stand outside in the rain while cops searched the building, but that was the worst of it: We got a little damp.

In college, whenever I saw the news about another boy,

another town, another gun, my first feeling was always sadness and my second was always relief. Because I was done with that. I'd made it through. Sometimes I thought, with wonder: *I survived.* I'd done my time, I'd paid my dues, I didn't have to worry about it anymore. As if my childhood exposure inoculated me against any future threat, like it was chicken pox.

In 2007, three weeks away from graduation, I was on my way to class one day when I heard on the radio about Virginia Tech. Seventeen wounded, thirty-two dead. The boy with the handgun had walked up and down the halls shooting into rooms full of students and professors hiding behind tables and doors. He took a break to mail a package of photos and videos and letters to NBC. He knew they'd want it. He'd seen it before. He was the same age as me: twenty-two, a senior, nearly done with college. He was in eighth grade when Columbine happened. He went through high school under that cloud. So had all the kids he killed. They all survived too, until they didn't. I was shocked, and ashamed that I was shocked. I cried so much that week. I kept thinking, *It happens here too?* As if I'd ever lived anywhere else but right here in this world.

Hell's Bells

"Please sit," said the man, so we did.

The room was small and gray with fluorescent lights and a half-moon of folding metal chairs. The man stood facing us. I remember so much about that night but almost nothing about him, just what he told us to do.

"Close your eyes," he said, so we did that too. "Now, think about this. If you died today, do you know if you'd go to Heaven?"

I opened my eyes just enough to peek around the room. Everyone else's eyes were closed, their faces set in concentration. From down the hall, where we'd just been, came the sound of people screaming. I closed my eyes again. "Good," the man said. "If you're not sure, raise your hand. Then open your eyes."

One last time, I did what he said. I raised my hand. I opened my eyes. I expected to see everyone else's hands up too. I did not. The moment I clocked this, two women appeared and knelt on either side of me like I'd just been hit by a car. The room was so small, where had they been? "Hi there," one of them said, not without pity in her voice, but not without excitement either. She was smiling at me. The other woman held a small, fat Bible, which she opened and tilted toward me, tracing one passage with her fingernail. "Please," she said. "Will you read these words out loud?"

I looked at her, then down the page, then back at her. She was looking at me. The other woman was looking at me. Everyone was looking at me. The woman holding the Bible blinked. I knew what I was supposed to do, she had just told me what to do, the words were right there on the page, waiting for me to speak them. Later—later that night, and throughout the rest of my life—I would wonder what those women thought of me. That I was struck dumb by fear and doubt, perhaps. That I was a wayward soul so far gone I couldn't even read a simple verse. That I was someone who very badly needed what they wanted to give me. And I would think of everything I wanted to tell them to make them see that they were wrong.

I would have told them about the old church, my grand-parents' church, the one where Papa preached his sermons and Nannie directed Vacation Bible School, where I stewed in awe all those Sundays, where I had my First Communion and played a Wise Man in the Christmas pageant. I would tell them that, okay, fine, after my grandfather retired from the priesthood, when I was ten or eleven, my family kind of retired too, started sleeping in more Sundays than not, didn't always make it to a service even on Christmas Eve. But it was fine, I was fine, because I had friends and my friends had churches of their own, and they were always inviting me along, and I was always saying yes, compelled by the same nosiness that made me love playdates and sleepovers, the chance to study the minuscule differences between our families' cable TV rules and bathroom soaps and breakfast offerings. And so I went with Joy to a red-brick Baptist church where we sat on white pews with blue velour cushions and watched a boy get dunked in what looked like a cattle trough. I went with Jaclyn to her big Presbyterian church downtown where we memorized Bible verses in exchange for full-sized candy bars. I went on the youth retreat with Amy's non-denominational congregation, where college boys with acoustic guitars led the Sunday worship service and everyone cried except me and I wondered, not for the first time, *Am I doing this right?* I wouldn't have told the women that, though.

I would have told them that it was a relief when my family started going to church again, somewhere a bit less grand than my grandparents' church but still comfortingly Episcopalian: big red doors, dark nave. Spring of my eighth-grade year, I was confirmed there, I stood up in front of the whole congregation in my new sage-green ditsy print B. Moss dress then knelt before the Bishop of the Diocese of East Tennessee who laid his hands on my head, blessing me, mashing my butterfly clips into my scalp. My sister and I were acolytes, dressing in our one-size-fits-all robes in the sacristy before services, processing in and out with the priests and the choir, sitting in little nooks on either side of the chancel, trading smirks across the way. I loved being part of it all but apart from it, but I loved sitting with the congregation too, on the pew with my parents, one family among all the others doing what they were supposed to be doing on a Sunday morning. I loved the Book of Common Prayer with everything inside laid out like a script, now stand, now kneel, now repeat after me. I loved the sound of everyone opening their books at the same time, the slap and rustle of pages and the mounting murmur of all the voices reading the same words at the same time. *Forgive us our trespasses, as we forgive those who trespass against us.* All those hissing esses, kind little snakes in everybody's mouths.

I loved Sunday nights when the youth group got together, eating Papa John's and drinking Diet Dr. Peppers from the ancient vending machine in the parish hall kitchen. Someone was always quoting Monty Python, someone was always vaguely planning a ski trip to Gatlinburg that never came together. One night we were rifling through the church library and somebody found an old VHS copy of a documentary called *Hell's Bells: The Dangers of Rock 'n Roll*. We watched it on an A/V cart pulled from a Sunday school classroom and laughed so hard we cried. I wouldn't have told the women about that. I also wouldn't have told them that, whenever I tried to pray on my own, I never knew what to say, I had never known what to say. Sometimes, kneeling at the altar after taking communion, feeling the pressure of the congregation at my back, I bowed my head and recited the alphabet in my head, or sometimes I just held my breath for as long as I could. Even at night, in bed, alone, it was hard to muster. Didn't God already know my thoughts? Didn't he know, at the very least, what I just wrote in my journal? Did I really need to spell it out for Him?

I had my doubts, but equally I doubted my doubts, and equally I just loved going to church. I loved the routine of it, the people and the building, the way it smelled. It made me feel good, but I wasn't sure, the way some people seemed sure, that it made me good. Almost everyone I knew went to church, but not actually everyone, like Marie and her sisters and parents, and in my estimation they were extremely good people, maybe even better than most. What about them? What about my parents and sister and I in our in-between years? Had our souls been in jeopardy? It never felt that way. I never got the sense that God cared, or even noticed. But these women had noticed, these women who were still kneeling next to me, holding that book, staring up at me with pity and wavering patience.

They were there to save me, but why was I there? Because still I had friends with churches of their own, still I was compelled by a chance to visit someplace new. In this case my friend was Cindy, she of the double-jointed finger, who I'd known for years before realizing our paths had probably crossed before we met in sixth grade, because her family went to the same red-brick Baptist church I once visited with my friend Joy, the one with the blue velour pews. She had probably been there the night I watched the boy get baptized in the trough, though she couldn't say for sure—that kind of thing happened all the time at her church, at Sunday morning services and Sunday evening services and Wednesday night services, kids of all ages and adults too. But not babies, which was funny because the Episcopal church seemed to baptize almost exclusively babies, white-dressed red-faced screaming bloody murder as the lightest dribble of holy water hit their foreheads. I'd long been aware that these differences existed between my friends' denominations and my own, and though it was often the novelty of those differences that compelled me to tag along, I was beginning to understand that to some people those differences weren't amusing trivia but actually quite profound—were, in fact, the difference between eternal salvation and burning forever in Hell.

At age fourteen, almost fifteen, the way this manifested in my life was that Cindy demurred when I invited her to my youth group's annual Halloween party (fortune teller, haunted maze, *Drew's Famous Halloween Party Mix* looping all night on a boom box). "But you should come to this thing at my church," she said. "It's sort of a haunted house, but not really. It's Bible-themed." I imagined a guy in a ghostface mask multiplying five Snickers and two apple ciders to feed the five thousand. I was sold even before she said, "Plus, on the way we're going to Ryan's Steakhouse."

Friday night, I rode with her youth group in a big white van to the all-you-can-eat buffet—glorious—and then to an abandoned strip mall off Highway 153. The wide parking lot, usually desolate, was packed. A dozen other big white vans were corralled off to one side, the teenagers and chaperones they'd shuttled in now forming a line that snaked through a maze of stanchions and nylon rope toward the entrance of a dark-windowed former storefront. A purple tent with the lightbulb logo of J-103, the local Christian station, rose above the crowd and giant speakers blared a poppy praise-and-worship song. Cindy rolled her eyes—I knew she didn't go for this stuff, I knew she still hung onto her Beck and Wallflowers CDs despite what her pastor said about the evils of secular music—but seemingly all of the other kids, hundreds of them, were squealing and laughing, hands in the air, swaying and singing along with their eyes closed, shuffling forward every few minutes as group after group was summoned inside the building. They all seemed to be wearing shirts printed with Bible verses or the names of summer camps with crosses in place of all the T's. Crosses dangled around their necks and from their wrists on delicate chains and woven hemp bands. I was wearing a T-shirt too, my favorite, an orange, perfectly broken-in Hawaiian Tropic shirt from the '80s. I'd almost worn my own cross necklace but had decided against it—the silver charm hung from a cord of purple beads that would have clashed with my shirt. Standing there, I realized I'd picked fashion over Jesus. I didn't know if he would care, I didn't know if I even cared, but I sensed some of the people in the crowd around me might care. I felt homesick and trapped and stupid.

Inside the building it smelled like sawdust and fresh

paint, and people were screaming. At the end of the first hallway was a dark room with a low stage built against the far wall. The lights came up to show a set decorated like a suburban kitchen and a family sitting at a table: mother, father, son. They were arguing. "Kevin, you're wasting your life with all this drinking and partying," the father said to the son. "Go easy on him," the mother pleaded. "No, he's right," Kevin sneered. "My life is a waste. At least you won't miss me when I'm gone!" He grabbed his leather jacket, stomped off the stage, and the lights went out. In the next room there was another stage, this one done up like the parking lot of a dive bar. A fake car was parked to one side. The lights came up and Kevin stumbled around with a fake cigarette in one hand and a real but obviously empty red Solo cup in the other. "Woo hoo, crazy party," he said. "Woo hoo," said the other actors, raising their empty cups. A guy in a leather jacket entered the scene. Kevin confronted him. They yelled at each other about drugs, "the drugs," who had them and who didn't. They had a staged fist-fight. Kevin threw the leather-jacket guy to the ground then ran to the fake car. He jumped behind the wheel and the sound of a revving engine blasted over the speakers. The car began to move, somehow, rolling forward very slowly, just as an actress in a miniskirt stumbled into its path. She threw herself onto the hood of the car then rolled to the ground with a wail. We heard a recorded screech of brakes and shattering glass, and then the lights went out.

The next room was a cemetery. Kevin knelt on the AstroTurf next to a styrofoam headstone carved with a woman's name. He was crying and held a little plastic gun. "What have I done? Why did she die but I'm still alive? I don't deserve to live. I'm going to end it all tonight." He stood and raised the gun to his temple. I braced myself for the sound-effect gunshot, but just then an actor dressed as

Jesus emerged from stage left. He had a real beard and a shiny brown wig.

"Jesus?" said Kevin.

"It is me," said Jesus. "Do not fear. There is hope left for you."

"After all the terrible things I've done?" Kevin said, agog. "I disrespected my parents. I drank alcohol and did drugs. I even killed someone. No, it's too late for me."

"It is never too late to repent and enjoy everlasting life. All you must do is accept me, Jesus Christ, as your Lord and Savior," said Jesus.

Kevin began to boo-hoo. "Okay. I accept you, Jesus Christ, as my personal Lord and Savior." They hugged. Jesus looked pleased. "Thank you!" cried Kevin. "Thank you, Jesus!"

The next room was entirely dark except for the beam of a flashlight that guided us toward a set of wooden bleachers. I couldn't see a thing but I could tell the room was a big one, the walls and ceiling far away, the air prickling with something weird.

When the lights came up, it appeared we were in Heaven. At stage right, Jesus (different actor, same wig) sat in a gold throne flanked by cotton-batting clouds. At stage left was a long, black tunnel. A woman was walking down it, backlit by a bright white light. She was a frumpy twenty-something, dressed in khakis and a pink cardigan. She emerged from the tunnel looking around in stagey wonder, and when she saw Jesus sitting there, she fell to her knees.

"Hello, Stephanie," Jesus said. "Your time on earth has come to an end. Now you sit in judgement before me."

"Oh, I've been waiting for this day!" Stephanie said. "Jesus, I've spent my whole life serving you."

"Have you?" Jesus said.

"Yes, Lord," Stephanie beamed. "I went to church twice

every Sunday and every Wednesday night. I led my youth group and taught children's Sunday school. I go to a Christian college. I only listen to Christian music, and all my friends are Christian too. I've kept myself pure and faithful so that one day I might be here with you!"

Jesus narrowed his eyes. "All these things are true, Stephanie," he said. "But I can see your heart, and I can see that you have not accepted me as your Lord and Savior."

"What do you mean? Everything I told you—doesn't any of that count?"

"I am sorry," Jesus said. "But the wages of sin is death."

"But!" Stephanie protested. She became frantic, wringing her hands. "But, but—!"

Jesus shook his head. The white light of the tunnel suddenly turned red and two men in black bodysuits appeared. They grabbed Stephanie under her arms and dragged her away as she cried and thrashed. "But I was a good person!" she wailed. "I don't deserve this! Help me, Jesus, save me!" She screamed all the way down the tunnel until we couldn't see her anymore and soon she seemed to be screaming all around us. Her screams were matched and then overtaken by a terrible hammering that rose up from below, an unseen mass pounding on the underside of the wooden bleachers—demons, maybe, or legions of previously damned Sunday School teachers. Cindy and I grabbed at each other, screaming too, pulling up our feet in case they burst through to snatch us, and still the demons pounded and now they screamed too, feral screams slamming against the room's distant walls, doubling and tripling, filling my ears and my mind until there wasn't room for anything else.

And then it was over. The silence was sudden and complete. Gasps from the group, nervous laughter. Then the lights came up and we were hurried out to make room for the next group.

Back in the hall, Cindy and her youth group friends wiped their eyes and took deep, steadying breaths. They were laughing—at themselves or each other, I don't know. I wasn't laughing. My head was ringing, my legs felt heavy and soft. I wanted to run away but I had no idea where I was, had no way to get home except that big white van out in the parking lot. And anyway, there was still one more room.

The last room was small and gray with fluorescent lights and a half-moon of folding metal chairs. The man stood waiting for us. "Please sit," he said, so we did. "Close your eyes," he said, so we did. "Now, think about this. If you died today, do you know if you'd go to heaven?"

I'd obliged his first two requests, grateful for the calm instruction, for anything to push out the screams still pounding in my head. But what was this? I almost laughed. In all my years of intermittent Episcopal church attendance, one thing had become clear to me—that this was an impossible question to answer. That this question was, in a way, beside the point. That it was how you lived that mattered, not what you believed or thought you knew. That it was a matter of trying—to be decent, to be honest, to be helpful to people in the world—and rarely if ever knowing that you'd tried enough. A daunting prospect with eternity on the line, I had to admit, but wasn't that part of the great mystery of it all? Now here was this man asking me if I was going to heaven. Maybe he was joking? Or trying to trick us? I opened my eyes, just a smidge. Everyone else's eyes were closed. No smirks, no signs of stifled laughter, just screams from down the hall. It was a trick question, it must be, and I knew the answer.

"Raise your hand," he said, so I did—proudly, like the star student I loved to be, unashamed of my cleverness, unafraid to be correct.

It was then that I learned that, to Southern Baptists, the question of whether or not a person would go to heaven was not impossible to answer. I had misunderstood Kevin and Jesus and the gun in the cemetery. I had forgotten poor Stephanie in her pink cardigan. The question was not beside the point; the question was the whole point. So here came the women with their smiles and their Bibles. The open page, the fingernail along the words. Their eyes on me. Everyone's eyes on me. The shame bubbling up and paddling me from the inside like the pounding screaming masses under the bleachers, the wrongness doubling, tripling. In the years to come, I would have a thousand conversations with those women in my head. Or something less balanced than a conversation, which of course this never was. I would witness to them the way they tried to witness to me. I would recite my entire ecclesiastical resume, every pew, every altar, every hymn. I would watch their eyes grow wide with doubts of their own. I would take all the shame they'd made me feel in that brief encounter in that gray room and make them feel it instead, heap it upon them, crush them under the weight of it, make them see, make them feel, make them know. I would knock loose something in them the way they knocked loose something in me, something they once thought of as immovable, some-thing they once held so dear, and try as they might they'd never be able to set it right again either.

This is a fantasy, tempting but pointless. It is not what happened or what would ever happen. In the moment, all that mattered was this: There was one of me and two of them and God's word was on the page and everyone was staring at me waiting for me to do what I was supposed to do, to say the lines, to save my soul. And instead what I said was, "Um, I think I misunderstood the question?" And I began to laugh and wave my hands, like I was clearing the air of some embarrassing whiff of sulfur. "I'm fine, actually! I'm fine," I kept saying, and the woman sat back on their heels. "I just misunderstood the question," I said again. This was a lie, of course, but how would they know? How would anyone know, other than me? And well, God himself—but I had a feeling he hadn't even noticed.

The Middle

It was the end of the month, the end of the year, the end of the decade, the century, the millennium, or really it was only some of those things, but something had compelled a critical mass of humanity to bypass the chronological technicalities and celebrate early, and celebrate hard. Maybe it was that unfamiliar two leading off that big round number, the string of zeros lined up like an appreciative exclamation: *ooo!* Or maybe it was the fact that a not-small number of people seemed to be worried or hopeful or outright certain that when 1999 flipped over into 2000 we would have no more need for celebration, or calendars, or even the concept of time, and some others were bracing not for total annihilation but a good bit of chaos, and still others were bracing not for chaos, exactly, but for the chaos of those who expected chaos. It was hard to tell who was who, who was joking, who was afraid, who was both joking and afraid.

If I'd been any younger, I might have been satisfied by the reflexive reassurances I received from the grownup realm. I might not have noticed all the news reports with their flickering monitor screens and the magazine covers with their green-glowing zeros and ones and question marks. I might not have noticed how sometimes even the eyebrows of my outwardly unflappable parents raised or lowered in response to yet another prognostication of telecommunications breakdown, societal collapse, nuclear meltdown. If I'd been older, I might have been able to fully commit, either all the way unbothered or all the way out of my mind. Instead I teetered on the strange fulcrum of fifteen, neither here nor there, not knowing or not-knowing, a brief moment of equanimity, mistaken at the time for apathy, to which I would spend the next fifteen years, and then a few more, trying to claw my way back.

That night I stayed home. I was aware that there were parties happening somewhere out there, parties I might have been told about if I sat with different people in the cafeteria, parties I might have gone to if I was an entirely different person, and in that way it was like most Friday nights. My mother made the Omaha Steaks we'd been given for Christmas from Nana's new husband, Bud. That summer, Nana had showed me the flats of canned goods they had been stashing away, just in case. Now I wondered if they were huddled somewhere, the two old newlyweds, praying, dreading a future where nothing was certain but an abundance of mushy green beans. After dinner, we watched TV: Peter Jennings, Bee Gees, ball drop. At midnight, a smattering of fireworks around the subdivision. In the morning, the numbers on my alarm clock were red and square as always. Out my window, the sun sulked behind white clouds. Downstairs, my parents were drinking Folgers at the kitchen table and Sarah was watching the Rose Parade. I felt relieved, and stupid for feeling relieved, but oh well, here we were—not for always, but enough for now.

Many years later, after Nana died, in her liquor cabinet the night after her funeral someone would find a dusty bottle of champagne with a label demanding "CELEBRATE! THE YEAR 2000!" and a stack of "HAPPY NEW YEAR 2000!" napkins. She and Bud hadn't been huddling, after all: They had prepped for the end of the world, and then they threw a party. Though well into adulthood by then, I would feel a flash of retroactive adolescent loser shame at how I spent that long-ago night, mail-order beef then hours on the couch with my family. Then I would think, *How strange to prepare for the best and the worst at the very same time.* And then I would think, *Well, what else is there to do?*

Grand Voyager

Before I could drive, I dreamed about it for years—literally dreamed—long, lucid brain-plays where I, a child, would slip into unattended cars and take myself careening down busy streets, barreling through stop signs and red lights, flattening pedestrians who popped up whole and unharmed in my wake, and then, whenever I wanted to stop, unfamiliar with the precise mechanics of brake pedals, I would simply crash myself into a building, climb out, and walk away. I woke up from these dreams exhilarated, tingling. I would recount them in detail to my family at breakfast. The deranged joy sometimes lingered all day.

And yet, when the time came for me to actually learn how to drive, I was taken aback by my parents' reluctance. In my mind, legal ability was functionally synonymous with legal guarantee; as a suburban American teenager, swaddled all my life in endless, sidewalkless asphalt, a drivers' license was my birthright, was it not? It was not. My parents punted my acquisition of a learner's permit from my fifteenth birthday in November all the way to the following June, which was the earliest opportunity for me to spend a week in a muggy, wood-paneled classroom at Haman's New Drivers watching drunk-driving PSAs and getting drilled on "the rules of the road" by a profoundly mustachioed instructor alongside a dozen or so classmates who I slowly realized weren't New Drivers at all, but Old Drivers looking to expunge various traffic offenses from their records. Even once permitted, my learning consisted of short, creeping drives to Winn-Dixie, my mother tensed in the passenger seat like a concrete statue of herself, and aimless loops around empty church parking lots that often ended in scraped curbs, yelling, and tears. I was baffled. Haman's had made driving out to be a matter of keeping your blood alcohol content below point-ten percent and your hands on the wheel at ten and two. The most I ever drank was a weekly sip of communion wine and I was gripping the wheel so, so tight. What were my parents worried about and also why was this so hard?

According to the State of Tennessee, I would be eligible for my driver's license on Wednesday, November 8, 2000, my sixteenth birthday, but as the day approached, I worried that I would never be eligible in the eyes of Ralph and Kathy Maddux. I nursed a secret fantasy of them waking me up that morning, revealing that their hesitation and consternation had all been a ruse, whisking me off to the DMV, and presenting me with my very own PT Cruiser. Sensing the unlikelihood of this scenario—but also not wanting to ruin the surprise, just in case—I developed a cover story, telling my family and my friends and anyone else who asked, and at least a few who didn't, "All I want for my birthday is a new President!" It seemed like the lowest of low bars: Election Day was the day before, and of course we would know the winner by the next morning. I didn't even care who won, didn't see much of a difference between Bush and Gore, might have joined my parents in shrugging and voting for Nader if I'd been born two years and a few days earlier. But it took five weeks and a Supreme Court case for even my joke-wish to come true.

It was never going to happen, and then of course it happened, in the spring and all at once. I was taken to the DMV, I passed my road test, I was granted custody of my parents' 1994 Plymouth Grand Voyager and a Nokia-branded brick. I got a job scooping ice cream at Baskin Robbins. I drove to Marie's house, I drove to church, I drove to Target to spend my paychecks on Kodak film and CDs, though "driving" never felt like the right verb. The van was a tank; it lumbered, it heaved. Sometimes, mashing the accelerator to get up a hill I'd never even noticed was a hill before, I wondered at how much force would be required to dent a brick wall, let alone crash all the way through one like I had with ease so many times in my dreams. On the way to work one afternoon, I stopped at a red light and checked my rearview mirror at the exact moment the car behind me got rear-ended. The force of impact lurched it forward but somehow not enough to hit me in turn, and then the light turned green and I continued onward, as if pushed, a startled robot on my little track. I was still shaking when I clocked in at Baskin Robbins, couldn't stop yammering about it to my stoned coworkers, flinched at every car approaching in my rearview all the way home and for days after. But I was doing it, I was doing it, I was moving myself through the world at last.

* * *

That summer, I began to suspect that everything had already happened. Not to me, of course—even with license in hand, I had plenty of happening left to do—but to America or the world at large or whatever. It was 2001 and we'd figured out everything we were ever going to figure out, we'd become whatever we were always supposed to be, we'd hit the outer limits of what could be experienced and recounted as fact to anyone who wasn't there when it happened. There was no history anymore, there was only the news. We'd hit the cruise control button on humanity, and unlike the one on my minivan, it actually worked.

It was under the influence of this hunch that I reported to sixth period on the first day of eleventh grade. The class was called American Studies; I'd been impatient for it since Freshman Family Night, when our tour guide, a pimply upperclassman, mentioned its existence. It was "interdisciplinary," he'd said—as if that was a word you could just *say*—history and literature, juniors only, excellent grades and a teacher reference required. Every spring, the class took a bus trip from Chattanooga up to Washington, D.C., Boston, and New York City. "We just got back a couple weeks ago," he'd sighed. "It pretty much changed my life." I could tell. I could smell the freedom on him—I wanted it on me too—and now, at last, it was time. American Studies met in the classroom of its literature instructor, Mrs. Ireland. She was petite with a dark bob and frosty eyes and a reputation for throwing books at smart-asses. History was taught by one Major Dean, a retired Army officer who ran the school's JROTC program, Mrs. Ireland's perfect opposite: alarmingly tall, reserved, his weapon of choice a withering stare over the top of his bifo-cals. Someone had affixed a small plaque over the doorway: "Abandon all hope, ye who enter here." I did not know what that meant but I was more than willing.

On the first day of class we received a strange docu-ment, something called a syllabus, an outline of what we would be learning and when we would be learning it for the next two semesters. If it had ever occurred to me that teachers planned their lessons, it certainly had never occurred to me that they might share the plans in advance. What a novelty—what a miracle?—to be able to look ahead and see where we would be next week, next month, next year. "We should hit Vietnam by May," Major Dean said, flipping to the final page, confirming my suspicion that history was over and placing its terminus well before my own birth.

"We'll be lucky if we hit the Red Scare," scoffed Mrs. Ireland.

"And if we're really lucky, *you* won't hit *us*," said my friend Dan, who sat in the second row despite being almost as tall as Major Dean. Everyone laughed, proud of ourselves for knowing the lore, giddy to see it in action. Mrs. Ireland made *I'm watching you* fingers at him—at all of us—before elbowing Major Dean away from the chalkboard, scrawling words I dutifully copied onto my blank notebook paper: CITY ON A HILL.

We started where America started, one version of it anyway. Mrs. Ireland led us through John Winthrop's sermon with all its intransigent vowels: *The eies of all people are upon us.* Major Dean held forth on the Puritans and their dreams of the so-called New World and the crushing realities on its shores. Weeks passed, August became September; we read Hawthorne and Poe and Emerson and Thoreau. Mrs. Ireland called all of them by their last names, and all of us by our last names too. The Puritans became the Colonists and the Colonists became the Revolutionaries and they spread down from the North and out from the East, South and West and West some more. They stole people, they stole land, they saw none of it as stealing, they saw all of it as theirs by right, by God, and still it wasn't enough. MANIFEST DESTINY, Major Dean scrawled on the board one day. HUBRIS, he wrote next and underlined it twice. Strange new words for those strange old American tendencies to think we always know best.

Every day I filled pages and pages with notes, my hand cramping pleasantly as I tried to keep up. We moved fast, two hundred years gone in a flash. We were set to begin our unit on the Civil War on the second Tuesday in September. Instead we sat watching the big television on the media cart, watching the planes hit the towers over and over again, just like we'd been doing all day.

It had started in first period, which for me was Psychology with Mrs. Webster, a class that, if it had a syllabus, would have included such units as "Dream Journaling" and "Watching *Sybil* Like It's A Documentary." I don't remember that day's lesson, but it ended when the classroom phone rang. "Hello?" Mrs. Webster said, then made a strange noise. She jumped out of her chair, hopped around looking for the remote control, tangled herself in the phone cord, and finally turned on the TV. "Oh my God," she kept saying, "Oh my God," flipping channels as my classmates and I sat entranced by her apparent malfunctioning. When she finally landed on CNN, the morning show anchors seemed very confused. They were trying to figure out what kind of navigation system failure would send a commercial airliner flying anywhere near the tallest building in the world, let alone close enough to hit it. I remembered my old dreams about driving, how easy it had been to crash, how fun; I remembered the fender-bender behind me, the sick crunch of it, the deep sense of wrongness that trailed behind me for days. They kept cutting to live footage of the towers in Manhattan, recognizable even to us down in Tennessee. There was a hole in one of the buildings and black smoke was seeping out. How strange. We saw the second plane hit. An eerie, brazen blur, then fireball, then more smoke. We watched until the bell rang for second period and we spilled out of the classroom into another version of the world.

Until that day I had never noticed how many televisions we had at school. There turned out to be one in every classroom and in the corners of the cafeteria and in the front office and all day we all watched the planes hit the towers over and over and over. We watched the buildings smolder and crumble and fall, and then they were whole again, just beginning to bleed. We watched the ash cloud drop, watched it flood ten blocks in as many seconds, watched the people stumble out of it gray as statues. Paper was flying everywhere, paper and ash and bits of horrible things. The first body collected from the rubble was that of a priest, white-haired like Papa. Behind every reporter, every red-eyed witness, every shaky camera feed, the endless wail of sirens beat against the walls of the city.

That night, the President who hadn't been elected on my birthday said, "They have failed. Our country is strong." By then I'd seen the footage of him hearing the news during story-time at the elementary school in Florida. The look on his face when the aide leaned in. The blankness. At least a light bulb usually flickers before it goes dark. I thought, *Oh no.* The next day, someone at school was handing out American flag stickers. I put one on my van. Where did they come from, all these flag stickers? Where had they been the day before? Had some factory been printing them just in case? Had they known what was coming? At school we already said the Pledge of Allegiance every morning, like we had since kindergarten, but now we said it louder, hands still misplaced over what we thought were our hearts. I heard boys talking about the draft, boys I'd never thought twice about, but now I ached for them. All their ears were too big and their arms too thin. Even the biggest football players suddenly seemed like soft-kneed toddlers. How in the world could *they* go to war? And what war, anyway? The President said we should go shopping and for some reason I did what he said. I deposited my final Baskin Robbins paycheck and went to the mall. I went to Dillard's and I bought an American flag tank top. I went to The Icing and I bought a chunky silver ring that said "ANTI." I wasn't sure what I was "ANTI" but figured I'd know soon enough.

Everybody was talking about God, even more than usual. What he did or didn't have to do with it. What he wanted us to do next. Sometimes I thought about the men who flew the planes into the buildings. (I knew they were men before we knew who they were—the men with the planes, the boys with the guns.) I couldn't imagine what it would be like to be so sure about anything. On TV, the piles of rubble smoldered and settled and shrank. The last live body was pulled from the pile and the first troops were sent off to Afghanistan. None were my classmates, at least not yet. The booster club hired a Lee Greenwood impersonator to sing the National Anthem at the homecoming game in October. At halftime, he returned for his rendition of "I'm Proud to be an American." Everyone sang along and cried. I thought it was so stupid but I was crying too. Because I used to be, because I wanted to be, because I didn't know what I was anymore. It seemed that we had taken everything for granted, or at least I had, especially whatever meant "we," whatever meant "everything." My sense of what was possible had simultaneously expanded and collapsed. Human capacity for evil was far more vast than I'd ever thought to believe, and whatever space I might one day occupy in the world had seemed to shrink by an equal degree. An unknown quantity of unknown somethings had been confiscated. The colleges I pined for were all in big cities, surrounded by skyscrapers, impractical to visit by anything but air travel. In American Studies we were barely past the Battle of Gettysburg but I remembered the little bit I already knew about the World Wars and Korea and Vietnam, all the boys who went off and never came home, all the women left behind. All the dead people everywhere, all over. The idea of a draft was terrifying, those numbers and their random fates; the idea that women wouldn't be drafted, or hadn't been before, was an appalling relief. I thought we were past this. I thought history was over. I thought we were free. I never knew it was possible to be this kind of wrong.

In the face of all these things I had no control over, I became obsessed with whether or not my class would still be able to go on the American Studies trip, which I also had no control over. That fall, that winter, anytime anyone asked if it was still happening, Major Dean and Mrs. Ireland said the same infuriating thing every adult seemed to be saying to every question about the future: "Let's just wait and see." But I was tired of waiting. All I'd ever done was wait. And wait for what? By spring, would there perhaps not be an America left for us to study? Maybe not, I thought, and maybe it would be for the best. I thought of the little wooden sign that had always hung in my house some-where, the one that said "Bloom where you are planted." Well, maybe I would. It was easy enough to imagine my life continuing and ending there in the city where I was born, the state I'd rarely left. Maybe it was better to let the rest of the world remain a tantalizing abstract. Better, anyway, than knowing it as something real, something possible, before having it snatched right out of my hands.

* * *

I didn't allow myself to believe the trip was going to happen until four-thirty in the morning on the last day of March when I sat in the second-to-last seat of a charter bus rumbling out across the school parking lot, watching my parents standing there with all the other parents silhouetted in their cars' headlights, all of them waving, all of us waving too, though the windows were tinted and they couldn't see us. Then the bus turned onto the road and, finally, we couldn't see them either.

We drove up through Tennessee and Virginia and into Washington D.C., the city a monument to itself, to every good and bad American idea, fallen cherry blossoms everywhere edging pink to brown. Later we would tour the foggy mansions of Newport and eat lobster rolls in Boston and stare out the bus windows at Amish country, sheep and dark-bundled children staring right back. But first we cut a path through Maryland and New Jersey until New York City appeared before us, bronze teeth glowing against a lavender sky. The Holland Tunnel sucked us in and spit us out into Lower Manhattan. Our hotel was around the corner from a Starbucks, the first I'd ever seen. We unloaded the bus and dragged our borrowed luggage through the lobby. The elevator smelled like pee and wheezed all the way up to the eleventh floor. The room my friends and I were assigned to smelled like pee too. Someone flipped on the lights and they all shorted out; someone pulled open the shades. The sun was shining somewhere nearby but not exactly here. We were unpacking in the semi-dark when I heard the first sirens go by. Hundreds of feet below, the sound doubled and redoubled by the steel and concrete building faces, they sounded nothing like our sirens at home. But something about them was so familiar. "Why do I feel like I've been here before?" I said. My friends shrugged. I wondered if it was because I actually *had* been there before, maybe in some other life, not as an eleventh grader on a class trip but someone else entirely, someone wise and worldly and unimpressed by chain coffee shops. Then another pack of fire trucks screamed past below and I realized their familiarity was nothing so cosmic. It was only the sound I'd heard on loop in the background all through the past six months of news.

We all met down in the lobby at six o'clock sharp. Mrs. Ireland called roll—a practice without which we would have left one kid at the hotel in D.C., another at a middle-of-nowhere Roy Rogers—then led us out into the city. It was twilight. At a subway station down the block we changed our money into little coins with holes in the middle then boarded a southbound train. We emerged onto the street in a steady, lacy rain. "This way, troops," Mrs. Ireland said. We followed her down the street like ducklings until someone realized we were going the wrong direction and we turned around and walked the other way for a while. It was getting dark now, and soon we saw the glow.

We could see it from blocks away. Up close, the solid glow resolved into component parts: spotlights, floodlights, all rigged to scaffolding and beaming down into an immense nothingness where the two towers had been. The buildings standing all around seemed impossibly tall on their own, taller than any back home for sure, all battered and boarded up with American flags stretched here and there like giant Band-Aids. Raindrops caught the light like snow. We'd all been talking as we walked, but now we shut up. We stood on the sidewalk outside an old church and took turns on an observation deck built along the empty street. Over there, a great big hole. Over here, paper everywhere, flyers upon flyers, stapled and pasted and papier-mâchéd by wind and rain. The outermost asked the same questions as the ones a dozen layers deep: HAVE YOU SEEN ME? DO YOU

KNOW WHERE I AM? Drifts of stuffed animals and silk bouquets, candles burned all the way down with rain shimmering in the sunken pits.

A low, bubbly feeling moved through me, collecting in my chest then spreading out along my arms and pooling heavy in my hands. I'd never felt it before but I would feel it again a few days later when we stood on the edge of a field at Gettysburg, the sky low and gray, the park ranger saying, "More than three thousand people died here in three days of fighting." I'd seen the old daguerreotypes—the field of fallen bodies, piles of dead boys all the way to the horizon— but it was something different to be standing there. The dark carbonation rose and scattered through me, like the feeling just before goosebumps pop up on your skin, only it was inside my body and never crested so I couldn't shake it away. I stood there staring at the towers' pitted basements. How many people had died somewhere in the air above me? How many bodies had been made invisible by flame and how many were pulled from the pile which was invisible now too? I'd known once but I didn't know anymore. I'd committed the new sin of forgetting. We were part of the great parade of history after all. It was so hard to keep up.

The next night we all dressed up fancy, boys in sport coats, girls in black dresses. Our bus took us uptown to Sardi's and after dinner we walked a few blocks over to The Imperial for *Les Miserables*. Inside the theater everything was red and gold and our seats were so high up in the balcony I got dizzy when I leaned forward. I cried my way through the show, just like I had every time I watched it on PBS's *Great Performances* since I was ten, and at curtain call I wasn't even embarrassed because everyone else seemed to be crying too. On the way downstairs, I was snared by the merchandise booth. The line was long but Mrs. Ireland said, "Take your time, Maddux," then hurried away as if I hadn't already seen her own raw eyes and runny nose.

I waited my turn, then bought a poster and a mug and ran downstairs to meet my classmates in the lobby. But the only people I saw were a few stoic ushers and a couple of grown-up couples composing themselves. I pushed through the big brass-handled doors but my class wasn't on the sidewalk either, and I didn't see them up or down the block. My instinct to panic was only slightly edged out by my instinct to believe I was wrong. Maybe we weren't supposed to meet in the lobby—maybe we were meeting back at Sardi's? In my black dress and unfamiliar heels I jogged down the block, turned down a wide alley, then rounded the corner onto West 44th Street. I expected to see the bus idling by the curb, everyone already in their seats, Mrs. Ireland leaning out the door screeching at my tardiness. But it was just taxis and hot dog carts and post-show, pre-whatever crowds barely registering my presence on their sweep down the glittering way. In the distance, sirens howled. I pictured my Nokia, too fat to carry in the clutch I'd borrowed from my mother, languishing on my bed back at the hotel. I pictured my mother finding out about this and covering her face, fake screaming in real horror. At home, I knew where all the streets would take me but only half of their names. Here, big signs told me what the streets were called but not where I was supposed to go. No one knew where I was, not even me.

I turned back toward The Imperial, hoping the ticket stub in my clutch and my sackful of merchandise would qualify me for sanctuary there or at least access to a telephone—to call who, exactly? A huge marquee blinked out C-H-I-C-A-G-O over my head. I turned back down West 45th Street, empty except for two cops leaning in a doorway. I heard Rudy Giuliani's voice in my head: *New York's finest!* I managed a prayer: *Dear God, please let them hear me scream when I get murdered or at least find my body before I start to decompose.* Ahead of me, a small marquee bore the image of Bea Arthur smirking in a blue caftan. *Dear God,* I amended. *Please don't let Bea Arthur be the last face I see before I die.*

I was half-running, half-walking, my heels rubbing my heels raw. I could see The Imperial and its stammering lights down the block. Then, as I got closer, breathing heavy, I saw them too: my classmates, all of them, standing on the curb where I'd looked for them first. They seem pasted in somehow, rendered by a different artist than the rest of the city. Rounder edges, brighter features. How could I have missed them?

Suddenly, I heard my name. "There she is!" shouted my tall friend Dan, and everyone turned to look where he pointed.

"Where'd you go, Maddux? Back to Tennessee?" Mrs. Ireland hollered, and my friends crossed their arms like disappointed mothers. I flung out my arms and ran toward them, laughing like I'd never been afraid of anything in my whole entire life.

Each to Each

My cousin Marie and I were good girls. Smart girls. Girls with good heads on our shoulders, which were also good. At my football-worshipping public school in the suburbs and her artsy-fartsy magnet school downtown, we raised our hands first in class, we carried group projects, we joined clubs, we stayed late after school and we liked it. We were Girl Scouts long after we wanted anyone to know that we were Girl Scouts. We took our PSATs and our ACTs and our SATs and diligently studied the reams of promotional materials subsequently mailed to our homes by seemingly every institution of higher education in the United States of America. We weren't our class valedictorians but we sat with them at lunch. We didn't smoke and we didn't drink, except Marie and the one bottle of Zima that one time. We drove the speed limit, me in my minivan and Marie in her wood-paneled station wagon. We were the kind of girls, I believed, who weren't supposed to care about boys. We were supposed to know better than to waste our time and energy on something so trivial, something so ephemeral, as romance. We were supposed to be above it. We were not.

It began, for her, with Harrison Ford in *Indiana Jones* and *Star Wars*; for me, with Christian Bale in *Little Women*. Next, for both of us, Hanson: Isaac for her, Taylor for me, Zac relegated to our little sisters. With real-life boys, the pattern continued. Our crushes were furtive, obsessive, and categorically unrequited. We had divergent tastes but a shared knack for liking boys that never liked us back, or at least always had girlfriends who weren't us. I suspected this was genetic, somehow; at the very least, it seemed like an appropriate punishment for our transgressions. We rehashed and rehearsed our suffering primarily in Marie's bedroom, which was in her family's basement and full of secrets: drawers and shelves crammed with obscure treasures, sliding closet doors barely holding back a landslide of old toys and art projects; walls scaled with posters and photographs and sentimental food wrappers. One of her high, narrow windows opened into a cinder block crawl space, onto one wall of which she'd painted a tropical island scene that you couldn't see unless you knew how to shine a flashlight in at just the right angle. But it was always there: wavy blue sea, palm tree dropping coconuts, orange-haired mermaid waving into the dark. An ideal oubliette for airing our mortifying desires. I would arrive in the morning and we would talk all day, make a brief appearance upstairs for sustenance, then retreat once more and continue talking all night, splayed on the floor or her inflatable couch, until we got tired and retreated to bed, the bunk bed I'd coveted since we were little kids, her on the bottom and me up top. She'd turn off the big light and turn on her bedside lamp, the one on which she'd written some of T.S. Eliot's "The Love Song of J. Alfred Prufrock" in Sharpie around the shade: *I have heard the mermaids singing, each to each. I do not think that they will sing to me.* Then we'd talk some more until one of us realized the other had fallen asleep.

Sometimes I forgot who were Marie's crushes and who were my own. It hardly mattered. There was something exquisite about our longing. We got so good at pining that getting what we wanted never could have compared. Or that's what I told myself. Now I see that we were making ourselves suffer so that nobody else could. Over the years, at our respective schools, we watched countless relationships progress through their natural life cycles, from sweaty hand-holding to gratuitous smooching between classes to steely avoidance. The prospect of a boy liking me back made me giddy; the prospect of a boy liking me back, then not liking me anymore, right there in front of everybody, made me want to become a Shaker. And then the only thing worse than the idea of breaking up was the idea of never breaking up. Both of our schools had a few long-running couples who were famous for being all but engaged, who traded dry pecks on the cheek when they parted in the cafeteria, who talked about each others' parents the way our parents talked about their in-laws—they gave off such an unsettling whiff of middle age, I kept my distance with the same diligence I avoided the shamelessly slobbering new couples. I wasn't aiming for rumor-mill grist or for a lifetime contract, I just wanted some floppy-haired boy to say he liked me and kiss me before I died.

* * *

For a while, most of our school friends seemed to suffer from the same self-imposed smart-girl spinsterhood as we did. But Marie's sixteenth birthday party, in January 2001, was infiltrated by a curious creature: somebody's actual boyfriend. Lindsey met Joe the summer before at swing dance camp, which to me implied a certain active, twirling interest in one another, but all night they sat a foot apart on

Marie's living room couch, vaguely holding hands, rarely looking at or speaking to one another. Meanwhile, everyone else worked their way through the kitchen table buffet of Sam's Club snacks and jockeyed for control of the stereo. Someone found the *Full Monty* soundtrack on Marie's parents' CD tower and everyone screamed. I watched Joe blush livid pink, or maybe his cheeks were always that color. Brown curls, freckle-splattered face. He was so cute, if I'd seen him somewhere alone I would have known he had a girlfriend. I stuffed another mini-quiche into my mouth as the guy from Hot Chocolate sang, "How did you know I needed you so badly? How did you know I'd give my heart so gladly?"

A few months later, like clockwork, Lindsey dumped Joe. "Apparently he's a bad kisser," Marie reported via AOL Instant Messenger one night. "But would it be weird if I stayed friends with him?" He was funny and smart, she said; he was a year younger than us, a ninth grader, on scholarship at the private boys' school downtown. He did theatre and mock trial and he was in a band. He had a LiveJournal. She sent me a link. He posted about listening to Bob Dylan and Radiohead and Pink Floyd and often listed his mood as "quixotic."

"Dunno if that's weird," I said. "But he does seem like he'd be a good friend."

"Okay," she said. "I'm gonna do it."

Down in her bedroom, Marie had a bulletin board where she tacked up photos of all her favorite people: her sisters, me and my sister, our boy cousins from California, Lindsey and her other friends from school. After a while she added a photo of Joe. I wondered if she had a crush on him. But that summer, when she told me he had a new girlfriend —some red-haired girl from another private school—she didn't seem sad. So why was I?

* * *

That summer, the one when I worked at Baskin Robbins, Marie spent six weeks across the state at the Tennessee Governor's School for the Humanities. She came home in July mutually smitten with a boy from Knoxville named Thomas. "He's a Marxist," she sighed. "And he looks like Peter Pan."

They were a dreamy match, aside from the hundred or so miles of I-75 between their houses. They talked on AIM every night and wrote mushy notes in their LiveJournal comments. He made her like Dave Matthews Band and she made him like Ben Folds Five. Sometimes I tested myself to see if I was jealous—of her, of him, of them. The answer was mostly no. Thomas was just a blue name on a white screen. Marie was happy as ever to stay up sorting through all of my futureless prospects, plus now we had new mysteries to unravel, like why hadn't Thomas tried to kiss her at Governor's School when everyone else was hooking up like monkeys in a barrel? Was she supposed to kiss *him*? If he was Peter Pan, was she Wendy? Or was she Tinkerbell? Meanwhile, I felt like Captain Hook and the blasted clock was ticking away. I'd always been skeeved out by the phrase "sweet sixteen and never been kissed" and I hated it even more when I was exactly that. That November, after I turned seventeen, I often thought about finding some easy mark (perhaps named Mark, there sure were enough of them) and getting it over with. Then again, Marie had a boyfriend and couldn't get him to kiss her. She could barely get him in the same room.

"Thomas keeps blaming his dad, saying he won't let him take the car to Chattanooga for the day," she said one night, after we'd retreated to our bunks. "But what if his dad's not the problem? What if it's *him*?"

By then it was so late and we'd been talking for so long, all I could manage was a groan. I lay staring at her bulletin board on the opposite wall. The photo of Thomas she'd pinned up was blurry, the perfect point of his nose lost amid the flashed-out white of his face. All the photos were terrible, actually. My bangs were thin and greasy, my shoulders hunched. Joe looked like a real dork, too. Marie had clipped his photo from a *Times-Free Press* story about a community theatre production of *Godspell* he starred in as Jesus. In the shot he was dancing, arms bent, brown curls tossed forward. Marie had gone to see the play and reported that he was good, and also that he'd broken up with his red-haired girlfriend. She also told me she felt weird because she liked hanging out with Joe more than she liked hanging out with Lindsey. I felt weird too because whenever I stayed over, no matter what other boys I'd just spent hours trying to comprehend, his funny face was the one I thought about as I fell asleep.

* * *

I was once quite vulnerable to coincidences, especially when they involved boys I had crushes on. Unexpected sightings in otherwise empty school hallways, down the cereal aisle at Bi-Lo, across the Hamilton Place food court— I reported every encounter to Marie and we prodded them from every angle, torturing the meaning into revealing itself, until finally I realized it all meant nothing. Because everywhere I went I saw someone I knew. I saw boys I liked, boys I hated, girls I knew, my sister's friends, my parents' friends, my aunts' and uncles' and grandparents' friends, old regulars from Baskin Robbins whose names I'd forgotten but whose orders seemed stuck in my mind forever. There was no conspiracy, no secret message, no fate—I'd simply been living in the same town doing the same things for seventeen years. I had seen and would continue to see all the same faces in all the same places over and over again until I graduated and moved away or died.

So the Saturday afternoon in January 2002 when my youth group went to see a community theatre production of *Joseph & the Amazing Technicolor Dreamcoat*, I wasn't entirely surprised to see Marie's friend Joe's name on the program. It was like, well, duh. He played Simeon, the oldest brother. For "Those Canaan Days," he wore a beret and sang in a goofy French accent and the audience howled with laughter. Afterward, I saw him in the lobby and for some reason said hello. It had been a year since Marie's sixteenth birthday party, but he remembered me too. His hair was longer now. I almost said so, but then I realized of course his hair was longer, it had been a year, but it wasn't that much longer so he'd had it cut at least once, but that didn't seem like the kind of thing you said to someone, let alone a boy you hardly knew.

Instead I said, "You did great."

"Oh yeah?" he said, pink under his freckles. "Thanks." His curls blocked his eyes, which was a strange relief.

It wasn't a surprise, either, a week later, when I showed up to my mock trial team's scrimmage against the private boys' school and realized that Joe was their lead witness. He wore a dark-gray sweater with a light-gray stripe across the chest, and during cross-examination, when I should've been watching for holes in his testimony, I found myself wondering how it would feel to press my body against his body and under what circumstances I might find out. His team beat mine and I didn't even care.

And it wasn't a surprise, though for other reasons, when Thomas bailed on visiting Marie for the umpteenth time on what happened to be Valentine's Day. "You wanna go see

Joe's band play at some church on Frazier Avenue?" she asked me, knowing I didn't have anything better to do.

The church basement was dark, a dozen card tables set with spluttering heart-shaped votives. The band had no drummer. Joe sang and played guitar. The stage was low and covered in orange carpet, and a wooden crucifix hung on the wall behind them.

"Is Joe, like, religious?" I whispered to Marie.

"I think he's whatever you are," she said. "Episcopalian-ish?"

The band played Neil Young and the White Stripes, then two girls went up and sang "Magic Man" by Heart. I found myself wondering if Joe would still like me when he learned I couldn't sing. Then I caught myself: *still?*

Back at Marie's house, I lay awake long after she switched off her Prufrock lamp. A constellation of glow-in-the-dark stars spun out across the ceiling three feet away from my face. I could feel it coming on like the flu, the ache in my joints and a hot weight in my head. A stupid crush. I knew exactly how it would go: weeks or months or years of agony, the feeling at the very sight or thought of him of all the air being pressed out of my lungs, the dumb pounding of the deepest animal part of my brain, the limpness of my tongue and steel clamp of my jaw, all that misery interspersed with just enough electric joy to trick me into thinking it was all worthwhile. All that, then one day he'd show up with a girlfriend who wasn't me and I'd feel that same old sinking sadness and I would have no one to blame but myself. Down on the bottom bunk, Marie began to snore. How had she done it? How had she met this boy and not only avoided falling in love with him, but in fact made him her friend? Were these feelings somehow optional? I'd never tried it before, driving them out of my body and mind, refusing them everything they needed to survive. But if she could do it, maybe I could too.

* * *

I gave it a try. Marie and I went to see our friend Joe's band play at the Battle of the Bands at Cricket Pavilion. We went to the zoo with our friend Joe then to The Mudpie where we all tried something called "hummus." When school was out for the summer we stayed up late talking on AIM, me and Marie and our friend Joe, clacking away about books and movies and weird old songs we downloaded on Audiogalaxy and our parents and our stupid schools and our dogs and our little sisters. We talked about God and whether or not he existed; they leaned toward no, and I realized I was no longer entirely sure.

In June, when Marie abandoned us for her family's annual month-long RV trip, Joe and I talked on AIM every night. And why not? We were friends with her and we could be friends without her. One night he asked me what was the next song he should learn to play on the guitar and I said "You've Got To Hide Your Love Away" by the Beatles. I didn't tell him that I was listening to it on repeat as a reminder to myself. I liked the way John Lennon said "Hey!" on the chorus, like he was barely stopping a friend from making a big mistake.

One night, Joe asked if I ever thought about how I wanted to die, like what my ideal scenario would be. "I dunno, I've never thought about it that way," I said.

"I'd want to be pretty old, like I'd have kids and grand-kids," he said. "And we'd have a big dinner one night, all of us together. Then I'd go sit in my armchair and fall asleep and I just wouldn't wake up."

"That sounds nice," I said.

"Sometimes," he told me another night, "I think I'll probably be miserable for the rest of my life."

"I don't think you will be," I said, but I didn't know why.

We decided to hang out in person, since that was something else friends did. We met at the Northgate Mall food court and I watched him eat Chick-fil-A. Then I drove us to Grumpy's where the used CDs were overpriced like always but among the books I found a cheap copy of Joseph Conrad's *Heart of Darkness*. I remembered it from one of his LiveJournal posts, about how we dream as we live: alone.

"That's a great book," he said when he saw it in my hand.

"Oh yeah?" I said, looking down like I was surprised to see it there.

I drove him back to his house and he said, "Wanna come in? My dad's here."

In the foyer, he bent to scruffle a miniature schnauzer who barked and barked and stared at me with buggy black eyes. Somewhere, unseen, his father smoked a pipe. I followed Joe down to the basement, then to a small, windowless room half occupied by a desk bearing a massive beige computer monitor and stacks and stacks of CD cases. A lamp glowed in the otherwise dark. He shut the door.

I sat in his desk chair, the same place he sat all those nights we typed at each other on AIM. He picked up his guitar. I didn't know where to put my eyes. I didn't know what would happen if I looked straight at him. He had a *Monty Python and the Holy Grail* poster and a Spirits of Rock poster with the dead floating heads of John Lennon and Jimi Hendrix and Jim Morrison. I looked up at them, then down at my hands.

He played "You've Got To Hide Your Love Away" and got the "Hey!" parts just right. He played a Radiohead song.

I couldn't tell a single word except a line of the chorus: "Just don't leave, don't leave."

I stared into the black eye of the guitar, and when he was done, I checked my watch. It was almost nine o'clock, the random curfew my mother had declared when I left the house that afternoon.

"I've gotta go," I said. He walked me to my car and waved as I drove away.

* * *

My plan worked, it worked so well, right up until it didn't anymore. Then all the feelings I'd been shoving away came oozing back and now they were triple-strength, making up for lost time. Whenever Joe and I were in the same room I could see a glowing strand between us, winding between all the other bodies, tying us together. When we weren't in the same room I wanted to know where he was and I wanted to be there too and if I couldn't be there then I wanted him to tell me all about it later. If I went a day without talking to him I felt blank and restless. When we did talk, even if it was just words on the screen, everything went gold around the edges.

When Marie got back from her family's RV trip I told her everything. She said, "Oh my gosh, this makes so much sense." Then she said, "You have to tell him."

I knew she was right but it seemed impossible. People told people they liked them all the time, but I couldn't imagine doing it myself. It felt cruel and reckless. Like one wrong move and everything would be blown apart forever.

Email seemed safest but I still cringed when I typed the words, imagining all the stupid girls who'd said them before: "I like you. Like, like you like you."

And later I cringed when I read his reply, bracing

myself for a blast of embarrassment and despair, but it never came. "I don't know what to say," he wrote, "except that lately I've been kind of feeling the same way about you."

I read it over and over again, at first because I didn't believe it, then because I believed it and had no idea what to do next. I'd imagined this moment, this declaration of mutual affection, so many times with so many boys before, but it had only ever dissolved into a blurry black hole; I had assumed that actually saying the words, even typing and reading them, would serve as an incantation of sorts, a magic spell that would reveal to me how to proceed. But it did not. Nothing happened. Nothing happened the day he emailed me back, nothing happened the day I picked him up and drove him to the music shop where he bought new guitar strings then we played frisbee at Coolidge Park. Nothing happened when I watched him eat a grilled cheese sandwich at River Street Deli, where he bit into the half-sour and said, "I love pickles," which I somehow already knew. Nothing happened the afternoon we watched *Plan 9 from Outer Space* sitting one foot apart on the old couch in his basement, though the schnauzer prowled and growled like she suspected something might. "Shh, girl," he said, and after a while she wandered away.

Nothing happened, and then school started again. It was my senior year and already I felt half gone. Why was I here? Why was I looking for him in the hallways? How had I never noticed all the boys in my classes were dreadful creatures? Even the ones I'd yearned after for years seemed like subpar knockoffs of their previous selves. There was one good boy in the whole world and none of these were him. None were Joe with his hair and his face and his arms and his crooked teeth. Joe, my friend. My friend who liked me too.

In September, a year after the day the planes flew into

the towers, I spent all day waiting for it to happen again. It didn't make sense, but it hadn't made sense the first time either. That night, by the time I was done with school and homework and dinner with my family, by the time I logged onto AIM, I was desperate for some kind of upheaval. I waited until Joe's screen name appeared on my BuddyList, and when it did I asked him what was going on.

I wasn't surprised to learn that there was another girl.

"It's not that I like her more than you," he said. "But I do like her, and I don't want to be dishonest with you."

"I understand," I said, and somehow this was true.

* * *

I fell asleep that night with my head full of burning buildings. I woke up and began the rest of my life.

I read *Hamlet* in AP English and dissected a cat in Anatomy & Physiology. I went to Model UN and Mock Trial practice. I learned how to crochet. I made one scarf, then another. I went to church on Sunday mornings and youth group on Sunday afternoons and I felt bad all the time about not being sure about God anymore.

I sent off college applications, just two: one to my dream school in Boston and the other to a school in Atlanta I begrudgingly considered in order to appease everyone who couldn't comprehend that Boston was my destiny. A bay-windowed dorm overlooking the Commons; a writing, literature, and publishing degree; a Dunkin' Donuts addiction— I could imagine it all with such clarity that I assumed it was my fate. But now I felt a sad twinge whenever I thought of it, and even when I thought of Atlanta, because wherever I went, I would be leaving Joe behind. And then another, sadder twinge, because he wasn't mine to leave.

I hung out with Marie. Marie and I hung out with Joe.

We were friends, after all. Still friends. We went to see his band play in the church basement and they opened with "You've Got To Hide Your Love Away" and summer felt like a long time ago.

I watched CNN at breakfast every morning. A sniper was at large in Washington, D.C. He shot a man walking across a Target parking lot. He shot a woman while she was pumping gas. People doing things I did all the time, dead by the distant hands of a man no one knew was there until he was gone.

I felt like I was running out of time. That's what I told Joe when I emailed him again in October, "I feel like I'm running out of time."

By then I no longer cared about the other girl and what he might feel for her. I knew how he looked at me and talked to me and how he'd cross a room to stand next to me. I knew he always stood closer to me than anyone else. I knew I let him stand closer to me than I let anyone else.

"I feel rushed and pressured to get as many things done as I can before college and if being with you can't ever, ever be one of those things, I need to know that," I wrote. I wasn't sure what I meant, but it seemed as good an argument as any.

It was a Saturday night. I sent the email then went with some school friends to a haunted corn maze. We walked through the rustling stalks with the purple sky darkening above. I heard the screams of hired ghouls setting upon the groups ahead of us, heard my own friends' screams as we walked into the same traps, heard screams that sounded like my own. But I wasn't scared, I wasn't even there. I was somewhere I didn't know yet. I was yes or no, I didn't know yet.

Joe didn't reply that night. He didn't reply Sunday morning or Sunday night or Monday morning. But when I got home from school on Monday afternoon, there he was in my inbox. And there were his words: "It can happen and it should happen and I would like it to happen."

I read his message over and over again until I was possessed by the strangest urge: to call him on the telephone. His sister answered, yelled his name, and dropped the receiver. When he finally picked up and said, "Hello?" I couldn't stop laughing.

* * *

That weekend I picked Joe up and we went to Arby's. I wanted him to kiss me, but not at Arby's, but I was still sad when he didn't. Then Marie called and told us to come meet her at Long John Silver's, so we did, but he didn't kiss me at Long John Silver's either. He didn't kiss me when I went to see him in his school production of *Flowers for Algernon* the day after my birthday. I was eighteen now and he was still sixteen and I wondered if that was scandalous. He didn't kiss me when we went to the Bijou to see *The Ring* but I did grab his arm a few times. It felt like a good arm. He didn't kiss me the day after Thanksgiving downtown at the Grand Illumination because he'd just had his wisdom teeth out, but we did hold hands as we walked around in the cold and he told me about all the foods he was going to eat when he could chew again. He didn't kiss me in December when I told him I got into my dream college in Boston, but that's because I told him on the telephone. He said, "Oh, wow." Then he said, "That's great, that's awesome," but he sounded sad and far away. And for the first time since I'd pulled the beautiful fat envelope out of my mailbox that afternoon, I thought of him and us and what it might mean. I don't remember when I told him that I got into my backup school in Atlanta, but he didn't kiss me then either. He didn't even kiss me at Christmas when I gave him the scarf I'd crocheted like Roger's from *Rent*, but he did give me his marked-up school copy of *A Streetcar Named Desire*. I thought about emailing him to ask when he was going to kiss me, but then I remembered I couldn't even breathe when our shoulders brushed. Instead, I read the play and imagined him as Stanley and me as Blanche until I realized, way too late, that definitely wasn't what he meant.

New Year's Eve, my friend Kelly, home from college, invited Marie and I to sleep over at her house. "Bring Joe too," she said, and I did, an arrangement her parents and mine and his all somehow approved of. Good girls, good kids, all of us.

Down in her parents' basement, we drank a lot of Dr. Pepper and played pool and watched Blockbuster rentals all night, long after midnight's confetti congealed in the Rotel dip. It was later than late when everyone began to fall asleep, bodies draped across various soft surfaces. Joe and I had brought our sleeping bags. I rolled mine out behind the loveseat and he rolled his out behind the couch. We lay down and our heads met at the corner of the L-shape. I lay there for a long time staring into the dark. When I held my breath I could hear Joe breathing and I could tell he wasn't asleep either. I held my breath for a long time.

Now it was 2003. On Valentine's Day, his band would play a show in the church basement again and I would watch him with a big dumb grin on my face, not wondering anymore what he'd say when he found out I couldn't sing, because he already knew and he said I wasn't *that* bad, really. Over spring break, my family would go to Pawleys Island again—the final family vacation of my childhood, as always spent in a rental house with no long-distance service or computer—and I would spend all week in a sulk, missing him. In May, I would drive us to prom in my minivan: me in a poufy blue dress, him in a costume tuxedo. A week later, he would sit through all eight valedictorian speeches at my graduation and, afterward, hand me a fistful of grocery store daisies. That summer, I would get a job selling tickets at the aquarium downtown and he would get a job at the Mellow Mushroom across the street and we would visit each other on our breaks, dashing over to say a furtive hello then dashing back, tourists thronging, clock ticking. And in August, I would leave for college, either a hundred and twenty or a thousand miles away, both distances equally incomprehensible to me then, in the earliest hours of that New Year's Day—incomprehensible and irrelevant, frankly, when in the moment he himself was so nearby, barely inches from me, barely a distance at all.

When he reached out and grabbed my hand it was like I'd made it happen with my own mind. He pulled my hand toward him then kissed it, once then twice. Elsewhere across the basement, everyone else was asleep or not asleep, hearing or not hearing our every smooch. It occurred to me that I should care, and then that I did not. Instead I felt around in the dark for his face. When I found it, I raised myself up on my elbows, hovered above him for a moment, then blindly smushed my mouth onto his. I kissed him once then twice then three times, four, five, maybe a hundred. Then I pulled away and buried my face in my pillow until I needed to breathe more than I needed to stop myself from laughing.

"I love you," he whispered.

"I love you," I whispered back. Then I thought, *I guess I can die now*. But I really didn't want to.

Unknown Unknowns

In March, my financial aid letters arrived and the United States invaded Iraq. Shock and awe, room and board, NATO, FAFSA, WMDs. I sat on the big plaid couch in my family's living room, thinking about the future —humanity's in general and my own in particular—as I watched the first bombs fall on Baghdad. The missiles were being launched, I knew, by artillery units nearby, but in the narrow scope of the CNN footage they appeared to be self-materializing in the night sky before tumbling down into the dark city, helpless against gravity, a manufactured inevitability that characterized the whole operation. I was tumbling too. The school in Boston, my dream school, had given me a single grant of $2,000, approximately enough to cover the cost of one nice winter coat and a few flights to and from Chattanooga. The school in Atlanta, my distant second choice, had given me half of a full-ride scholarship. For months I'd been bracing myself for these eventualities— the money, or the lack of money, and the war too—but still I was crushed, and embarrassed that I was crushed, though not embarrassed by the conflation of my personal academic fate with that of the however many thousands of people who now had to die because their country had bombs, or oil, or the wrong god. The reasons kept shifting. The stakes remained unequal. But I was eighteen. There was what I knew, and there was how I felt. And it all felt the same to me.

"It's your choice, honey," my parents told me, and I wanted to believe them, but every night after dinner they stayed at the kitchen table, talking in low voices over various stacks of papers, going silent and giving me wide, flat smiles whenever I passed through the kitchen on the way from ranting about the war with Marie and Joe on the computer to watching the war on TV. The President and his advisors reminded me of my school principal and all his vice principals. The war was like our safety drills, something they said was to protect us, but I couldn't see how, and I couldn't quite believe they believed it either. Were they lying, I wondered, or were they just stupid? And which was worse? An American soldier—a girl, or a woman, or whatever I was; she wasn't much older than me—had been wounded and captured by Iraqi troops and then rescued by U.S. special ops, pulled out on a stretcher with an American flag bunched up around her like a little kid's blanket. She'd joined the Army so she could afford to pay for college. I wondered why she hadn't just taken out some loans. Then again, I didn't really like the idea myself. Being in debt seemed like another kind of hostage situation—bloodless, but with ever-accumulating interest, and no buzzcut guys in desert fatigues to get you out. You had to become your own buzzcut guy in desert fatigues, and it might take the rest of your life.

In the end, I picked the school in Atlanta. I allowed my choice to be understood as pure financial prudence—and it was true, of course, that now I would only be going into a little bit of debt, rather than a huge amount of debt. But I let money stand in for all the other factors, which I felt I shouldn't care so much about, and yet I did: the prospect of winter in New England, the distance from Joe, the inaccessibility of home. The extremity of it all was unfathomable to me. And there was the question always clanging in my head, vague and portentous: What would I *do* if something *happened?* Planes flew into buildings, bombs fell on cities; some little animal part of my brain wanted me to stay close, lay low, play it safe. So I would.

On May 1, the day my enrollment deposit was due, I watched on TV as the President stood on an aircraft carrier off the coast of San Diego and gave a big speech saying major combat operations in Iraq were over. Behind him, a massive banner said "MISSION ACCOMPLISHED." But nothing was over. It had barely begun.

* * *

That summer was one goodbye after another: goodbye to my friends, my grandparents and aunts and uncles, goodbye to my church, goodbye to my minivan, goodbye to every familiar street and store and hill and tree. Goodbye to Sadie, old Buster's successor who was now getting old herself. Goodbye to my family's Compaq Presario and the lurid screech of its dial-up internet; now I had my own laptop and, soon, an ethernet connection. Goodbye to Marie, who was off to a hippie college in Western Massachusetts where they didn't give grades. Goodbye to Joe, who had his senior year of high school yet to go. Goodbye goodbye goodbye! I said my farewells like I would be making the trip down I-75 and never coming back, as if the ability to easily come back wasn't a leading factor in making the trip to begin with. My last night in Chattanooga, I put on a burned Joni Mitchell CD and sobbed. "You can't return, you can only look

135

behind from where you came," she sang—round and round, up and down. I'd always thought of myself as provisional, a placeholder for whoever I would one day become, and I always assumed college would be the place where I did that becoming. I'd craved that change, I was desperate for it. But now I was on the cusp—the eve of the first day of the rest of my life—and all I could see was everything I had to leave behind. And for what? To become who? I wanted to live somewhere new, I wanted to learn new things in a new way, but I did not want to *be* new, I just wanted to be myself.

In the morning I hauled down to Atlanta every book I owned, plus my childhood bookcase, and upon arrival in my fourth-floor dorm room began to decorate the cinder block wall over my extra-long twin bed with hundreds of snapshots I'd been collecting of my family and Joe and Marie and my closest high school friends and my less-close high school friends and a number of people I actually would have gone out of my way to avoid in public, but I knew them, I had known them, they were somehow part of me. In the days after my parents and sister and I said goodbye in the scorching parking lot, all of us sweaty and crying, I proceeded to phone home with such diligence that my mother finally said, "You know, sweetie, you don't *have* to call us every day." She was right, of course. I didn't have to call, I didn't have to ask what they were up to; I already knew. If it was, say, seven o'clock on a Friday in late August, I knew that my mother was cleaning up after dinner and my father was mowing the yard and my sister was downloading music on my Audiogalaxy account and Sadie was hunting voles in her pen, exactly like they always did, everything just the same, except I wasn't there, they were doing it all without me. This was what I'd always wanted to happen, if not exactly where, but for all the hopes I'd pinned on college as a transformational paradise—a reward at the end of a good life, not unlike Heaven itself—I'd never considered that getting there might require something that felt a little bit like dying.

That semester I took a class called Narratives of the Self, a requirement for all freshmen, part of the Core program the school was quite proud of. We began with *The Odyssey*. At first I read it diligently, literally, tracking the story with my yellow highlighter. But my section was taught by a professor from the philosophy department and plot was, apparently, beside the point. His primary academic interest seemed to be showing how everything was actually several smaller things, words especially. *NOSTOS*, he wrote on the board one day, and then *ALGOS*. "Greek for home," he said, "Greek for pain." He underlined the words, then wrote another underneath: NOSTALGIA. "The *pain*," he said slowly, as if allowing us time to shoulder the full weight of his pronouncement, "of going *home*." Somehow, by the end of the hour, we were all explaining to him that, yes, it *was* painful, and it was painful because it was *impossible*—in the coming and the going, and even in the staying, a place was always changing, a person was always changing, the future was always becoming the present, the present was forever slipping into the past—as impossible for us now as it was for Odysseus, as it was for whoever Homer had been. (As it was for Joni Mitchell too; round and round, up and down.) The professor leaned against the desk with his arms crossed, nodding sagely, as if considering these ideas for the first time. The gravitas of it all was undercut by his resemblance to Jeff Bridges in *The Big Lebowski*, but still I shivered in my seat. I'd thought nostalgia was just the feeling I got when I saw an old orange Volkswagen Bus or smelled fresh-cut grass. And it was still that. But it was also, I realized now, the leading condition of my whole entire life. This is what I wanted to learn. This is how I wanted to learn it. Of course I would change. Of course I would become someone new. It was only, like everything, a matter of time.

* * *

My roommate also had a boyfriend back in her hometown. We both had pictures of ourselves at prom, five months or five hundred years ago. I put mine in a frame on my desk: Joe and I under the arbor in my family's yard, neither of us looking at the camera or at one another. My roommate taped a poster-sized collage to the wall over her bed. Her boyfriend had a shiny tux and freshly frosted tips. The collage fell down one night when half the girls on our hall were piled into our room and my roommate was telling everyone about how she spent all her graduation money on cocaine and now she had a hole in her septum. "Oh no, it's a sign!" one girl gasped and everyone laughed. My roommate taped the collage back up but by morning it had fallen down again. She taped it back up again, and kept taping it back up for weeks, until one day she didn't. By then she was spending most nights in some guy's room on the second floor. "He's got this goose-down mattress topper, you know?" she said, but I also knew his roommate had a girlfriend with a single room across campus.

This was bad news for the guy with frosted tips, but great news for me. It meant I had the room to myself every night at nine o'clock when my cell plan's unlimited nights-and-weekends minutes kicked in and I could call Joe. I could picture this too: the cordless ringing in the kitchen, his sister sliding in sock feet on the tile floor to answer, him scrambling up from his basement lair to grab the receiver. I'd lay on my bed under my wall of photos, so many of the faces his own, and tell him about my classes, about the articles I was writing for the school newspaper, about the diminishing charms of the dining hall. He would tell me about band practice and play practice and all the Ivy League schools his college counselor was pushing that he knew he couldn't afford. I would hold my cell phone to one ear with one hand, then the other ear with the other hand, then with one shoulder and then the other until my neck felt weird, and then I'd just lay there with the phone balanced on the side of my head, trying not to imagine all the cancer cells going to seed in my brain.

When Joe and I talked on Friday nights, I always had to plug my free ear against the ruckus of the girls on my hall getting ready to go up to Greek Row, where the beer smelled like hot pee and the mixed drinks stained their teeth red and weird guys always tried to grind on them and mean girls gave them the stink-eye, and all of this was somehow the point. I liked having an excuse to stay behind, but sometimes Joe would say—probingly, mischievously—"Are you going with them?" and then I liked having an excuse to go. I would follow my friends across campus and down into the basement of one of the fraternity houses, then find a spot against the wall where I could hover for a while as the party moved around me, bodies in the dark motorized by Lil Jon saying "Yeah!" over and over again, hands clutching Solo cups like each one was the Holy Grail. There were twice as many girls as boys and everyone seemed a little bit wide-eyed, a little untethered—not just drunk but loosed from time, from whoever they'd been just weeks before. They were shedding their former selves, talking different, laughing different, somehow wearing their old clothes different. Brown hair became black, blonde became blonder or blue or purple. Eyebrows were pierced, and nostrils, and lips, and parts of faces I didn't even know had names. And the timorous newness of it all clouded the basement, burnt and sweet, like the clove cigarette smoke that plumed in from the front porch, and the back patio, and the windows that opened as the night went on, slowly replacing the air of the house itself.

Everyone who arrived with a boyfriend or girlfriend back home seemed to be decoupling now, actively or passively. Everyone was becoming new and meeting new people who were also becoming new, double new. And I had to admit there was something thrilling about the existence of all these new boys. They could be anyone, and with them, I could be anyone; a few quick, bold moves could knock my life onto an entirely different track. But their appeal was abstract, hypothetical. Up close, they were cardboard cut-outs with stuck-on googly eyes. Joe was more real in his absence than anyone I met in the flesh, and I was real to him too, real and known and loved. Despite my years of desperation for change, despite what I now knew of change's inevitability, I wanted to be with him, and I wanted to be the person I was with him, more than I wanted to be with or become anybody else.

* * *

In those first few weeks away, I thought often of Odysseus's wife Penelope: steadfast, weaving her tapestries, rebuffing her suitors. I thought of myself in her place, I took her prayer to Artemis as my own: "Strike me, so that I could meet the Odysseus I long for, even under the hateful earth, and not have to please the mind of an inferior husband." But I was not Penelope, stranded, waiting. I was the one who had left. I was the one who had to go home.

Odysseus was gone for twenty years, ten at war and ten trying to get back, before the Phaeacians helped him home to Ithaca disguised as a beggar, before he was recognized only by his old dog Argos, who wagged his tail once then died on a dung heap. I was gone for a month before the Friday afternoon in September when I caught a ride with a classmate up I-75 and dragged my laundry basket down the driveway to the house that had once been mine, and kind of still was. "Howdy, stranger!" my father said when I came through the door. My mother and sister came at me squealing. Sadie, no Argos, jumped up to greet me then ripped a room-clearing fart. I almost cried, and only partly from the stench. In the morning, running errands with my mother, I nearly cried again as I fought the urge to throw myself prostrate over the threshold at Walmart, so relieved was I to be anywhere I'd been before.

That night, I drove my old minivan across town to Joe's house. I rang the bell and he flung open the door. I'd almost forgotten he wasn't just a photograph, wasn't just a voice on the phone—no, he was real, real eyes in a real face, real arms that wrapped all the way around me and picked my feet up off the floor as the little gray schnauzer hopped around barking at me, even when Joe began pretend-strangling me and I began pretend-calling for help. We ate dinner with his family and then his parents and sister conveniently disappeared so we watched a DVD of *Rust Never Sleeps* on the big TV in the living room and made out a little bit. And then I began to cry.

At school I felt like myself, too much like myself—unchanged and unchangeable, incapable of transformation—but now, among so much acute familiarity, I felt suddenly alien, no longer trapped inside myself but hovering somewhere just beyond, skinless and bewildered. For weeks I'd been missing Joe and now here he was and it was everything I wanted, but also I missed my family and wanted to be home with them after being gone so long, and now I was gone from school and missing that too, wondering what the girls on my hall were doing without me, even though if I'd been there I probably would have been talking to Joe on the phone wishing I was wherever he was, which was right here with me.

I kept crying and Joe kept asking, "What's wrong? What's the matter?" and all I could say was, "I'm sorry, I don't know, I'm so sorry." Then I remembered I was happy, actually, and I started laughing and he started laughing too. "If you knew how much I loved you," he said after a while, "it would be creepy." Then I cried and laughed some more, because I did know, and it would have been, if I'd been anyone other than me.

* * *

Back at school, back in my new-old life, campus morphed into an autumnal cliché: blue skies, flaming trees, syrupy light. *The Odyssey* gave way to *Don Quixote* and St. Augustine's *Confessions*. (Women, it seemed, were not Selves worthy of Narrative.) Every week the newspaper came out with my name in it somewhere. For Halloween I dressed as an alien cheerleader and went with the girls on my hall to a party where a squad of sexy cops danced on a table to "Bombs Over Baghdad" and I decided that if anyone handed me a drink I'd take it. Nobody did, and I left early to walk home with an over-served Margot Tenenbaum who kept stopping to barf in various bushes, but that was exciting in its own way, drunk-adjacent still the wildest I'd ever been. Maybe this is how I would change, I thought: slowly, just slowly, so it wouldn't bend me double and come back up in a nasty pink rush.

I would never have much in the way of school spirit, but I did develop a certain affection for my college's mascot, the Stormy Petrel. It was a type of seabird apparently admired by the school's namesake, the eighteenth century British colonial governor of Georgia, for their determination to fly toward land even during the nastiest storms—so determined, my classmates and I were told, that sailors would often catch the birds, light their oily feathers on fire, and release them back into the howling night so they could follow the burning beacons back to shore. Accordingly, the school's Latin motto was *Nescit Cedere*—"he does not know how to give up." It was intended to be inspirational, this idea of these birds persevering through harrowing atmospheric conditions and overt human cruelty. We were meant to follow their example, but to me they seemed miscast as creatures worthy of reverence. The petrels were not practicing perseverance. They did not think of themselves as steadfast or patient or brave, as "giving up" or "not giving up." They did not think of themselves as being or doing anything. They were just birds, flying home. And sometimes, I had to imagine, flying *away* from home, out to sea, because that's where the food was. Either way, they kept flying because that's what they did, that's what they always did, that's the kind of bird they'd evolved to be. Whichever way they were flying, to home or to the sea, they were always flying away from the same thing—away from death—and of course they always made it, until they didn't. This is what I liked about them, not that they were remarkable but that they were so ordinary. They were only doing what any other animal would do, what we were all doing, just trying to steal back a little bit of oblivion.

* * *

After months of talking on the phone every night, Joe and I became minutely attuned to the tones of each others' voices. I could divine the quality of his day from how he said hello.

One night in December, just before finals, he picked up with a dark, flat, "Hey." This was new. I didn't like it.

"Hey," I said back.

"So my grandmother's sick," he sighed. "Like, really sick." This was his father's mother, curly-haired and stoop-shouldered, his last living grandparent. I'd met her only once—in passing, after one of his plays—but Joe had told me all about her, though now all I could remember was that when she looked after him as a baby she'd played so much Ray Charles he was singing "Hit the Road Jack" before he spoke in full sentences.

"Oh," I said.

"Yeah, she went into the hospital for a kidney infection the other day and now she has pneumonia." He sounded very tired. "I'm not sure she's gonna make it."

"Oh God," I said. I sensed there was some adult protocol that should be followed here, but I had no idea what it might be. "I'm sorry?"

"It's okay," I wanted him to say, but he didn't.

After we hung up I sat on my bed for a long time. Something was creeping in, a heavy low hum, familiar but distant but coming closer. "Oh God," I said again to my empty room. I knew it now. It was fear. That old fear, that old need to run. But why? I was a hundred and twenty miles away and she wasn't even dead, she wasn't even mine, she had nothing to do with me. Nothing at all. I didn't have to run; I just had to write my final papers and study for my exams, I had to buy Christmas gifts at the school bookstore and get to the dining hall where the professors were serving breakfast for dinner, I had to make one last appearance at one last party, I had to pack for home, I had to get a ride home, I had to unpack, do my laundry, wrap my presents, eat dinner with my family, drive around alone at dusk watching all the houses' Christmas lights flicker on. I had to, so I did. And every so often, just to be polite, I tried to say a little prayer: *Please don't let Joe's grandmother die.* I said it for her sake, and I said it for him, but mostly I said it for me.

It didn't work. She died anyway. When Joe called my parents' house to tell me, he sounded sadder than I'd ever heard him. I don't remember what I said.

The next day, some soldiers pulled Saddam Hussein out of his bunker in Iraq. The war was over but still it wasn't over. My mother conscripted me to help her decorate for Christmas. We were watching CNN and unpacking a box of Santa Claus figurines when Joe called the house again. "My grandmother's visitation is tomorrow night," he said. "Can you come?"

"No, I'm sorry, I don't think so," I said automatically, like he was a telemarketer and I was perfectly satisfied with my long-distance service.

"Oh, well, okay," he said.

I hung up and turned back to my mother and all the Santas in their bubble-wrap cocoons. I unrolled one and set him on the shelf. His eyes twinkled with reproach. I began to cry.

My mother, another Santa in her hand, observed a careful silence. Then she said, "I think you should go."

"But I *can't*," I wailed. "You know how I am."

"I do know," she said. "And I think you should go."

I began to cry harder. I wasn't just sad, I wasn't just afraid; I was also realizing that I was wrong, very wrong, and had been for quite some time. All those years ago, the night before Grandaddy's funeral, when my mother let me make my own choice, to go or not to go, and I chose not to go —was it possible, was it really possible, that in my mind this choice was somehow binding and universal? That being excused from this one particular funeral meant I would be excused from all other funerals for the rest of time, maybe even my own? Or maybe I'd been wrong even longer than that, since the fish died and the dog died and I refused to see what became of them. I'd always been allowed to run, I'd always been allowed to refuse. The way kids got bumpers at the bowling alley, the way girls got to do push-ups with their knees down—just if they wanted, just if they needed. Now, it seems, the offer had expired. Or been outgrown.

"But I can't," I said. "I can't, I can't, I can't."

"You can," my mother said.

I was agog. The nerve of this woman! Was this not her fault? Had she not been the one to give me that first free pass, and the second and the third and the fourth? And now, what—did she think I was somehow *less* afraid of death now than I was back then? Because I sure wasn't. I was maybe even *more* afraid, or at least more aware of all there was to lose, all the words I didn't know, all the stories I hadn't read or written, more keen than ever to keep flying between the sea and the shore, more resentful than ever of any reminder that one day it all had to end. Why did she think I could do this? Who did she think I was? Did she know something I didn't?

Well, of course she did. She was my mother. I was nineteen. I felt so stubborn in myself; I did not know how to give up. But she had only ever seen me change.

"It will mean a lot to Joe's parents," she said finally. "And to him."

I paced around the living room, stepping around boxes of wreaths and candles and even more Santas. How did we have so many damn Santas? I was flailing around for any excuse. Like maybe *I* would die so they'd all have to go to my funeral instead. But it was hard, now that she had invoked him, not to think of Joe. Not just a photograph, not just a voice on the phone. I loved him. I hated this. But I loved him.

"Okay, well, I *would* go," I finally spluttered. "But I don't have anything black to wear!"

My mother made a strangled noise and set down the Santa she'd been holding. He wobbled briefly, then steadied himself. "You don't have to wear *black*," she said. "Wear anything you want. And I'll drive you. I'll sit in the parking lot. You can call me when you're done and I'll be right there. You won't have to stay a minute longer than you want."

She looked at me and I looked at her, and the Santas looked at both of us, and finally I said, "Okay."

* * *

The next day in the back of my closet I found a pink turtleneck sweater and a pair of black dress slacks I'd worn to my senior year Model UN conferences. That seemed like a very long time ago but the clothes still fit me. Downstairs I put on an old gray peacoat, one I'd once imagined wearing in Boston. My mother drove me across town as the sun set into the blue December five o'clock. At the front door of the funeral home a man in a dark suit asked me who I was there for. I realized there was more than one dead person laid out somewhere inside. I realized I didn't know Joe's grandmother's name. Beyond the man, I could see a hallway with a series of numbered doors, like the set of a horrible game show. I thought of turning and running back to my mother's car—but then Joe was there, button-down shirt and necktie tucked under his sweater, cargo khaki pants I knew his mom bought him from Aeropostale, striding toward me in his worn brown loafers.

"Hi," Joe said.

"Hi," I said.

I wanted to walk into his arms, walk into his body, make

him make me disappear. Instead I followed him down the hall to a room where we joined a line shuffling toward a shiny brown casket, closed lid piled with red roses. The line deposited us in front of his parents and I said, "I'm so sorry." His father smiled and his mother said, "Thank you for coming. It means so much that you're here." My mother was right. How had she known?

Everyone in line ahead of us kept going toward the casket. I turned away and Joe followed me back into the hall. "Is it okay if we sit out here?" I said. "I need a minute."

"Yeah, sure," he said.

We plopped down on a bench. The walls were beige but everything else was dark blue, forest green, ferrous red. Not exactly cheery, but certainly nothing like the ghastly grim Hooper-Huddleston chapel I'd been imagining since Grandaddy died; probably that place looked much the same as this one. I felt a burble of old guilt that I hadn't gone to that funeral, that I'd left my sister to brave it all alone. I felt a burble of new guilt that I'd almost done the same tonight with Joe. And why? I was afraid of death, but what did that even mean? Nobody had ever asked me to explain myself, not then and not in all the years since, and I couldn't imagine what I would have said. But maybe if I'd been nudged just enough, at just the right angle, then I might have been able to articulate something to which someone could have offered some perfect counterpoint, some obviating reassurance. Maybe my whole life would have been different. Probably it would have, at least a little bit. But now it was like considering my life in Boston, or my life without Joe—not entirely impossible, just pointless, pleasureless. I was here now. Just here.

For a long time, Joe and I sat there on the bench and watched the visitors come and go. After a while I realized that I was still wearing my peacoat. "Ugh, so sweaty, I'm dying," I muttered as I shrugged it off, then began to sweat more when I realized what I'd said. Joe didn't seem to notice. He was sad but I couldn't tell how much exactly. His eyes always looked a little bit sad anyway, even when I knew he was happy. It was something I liked about him. I liked so much about him.

Two old ladies came down the hall and Joe introduced me to them, his great aunts. They each extended a hand to me and smiled a little smile, friendly but measured, like they didn't expect to ever see me again—a reasonable reaction, perhaps, to meeting their teenaged great-nephew's teenaged girlfriend. *I'm for real!* I wanted to shout. *I'm forever!* But I just shook their hands and smiled too, and then they shuffled away.

Now Joe turned to me and said, "I'm glad you came."

"Me too," I said, and it was true.

Lux Nova

Junior year, spring break: Paris. My Art History class flew overnight from Atlanta to Charles de Gaulle then immediately boarded a tour bus so cumbersome, so ostentatious—so embarrassingly American —I was shocked that they let us into the city. It barreled through town, down the Champs-Elysées and around the Arc de Triomphe and past the Eiffel Tower. Our local guide, a woman named Yvonne, stood swaying behind the driver. She had a triangle of frizzy copper hair and looked somewhere between thirty and seventy years old. The bus maneuvered through the Latin Quarter until it couldn't go any further. The streets were cobblestone, narrow but passable if not for the police barricades.

"The students are rioting," Yvonne said with a shrug and bounced off the bus.

We followed her up the block. All the shop windows were boarded up or busted in and through the shattered glass I could see trashed display cases, broken furniture, tangles of colored wire hanging from holes in ceiling tiles. On the corner, a Gap store (they had Gaps here?) looked like it had recently been on fire. I saw the same spray-painted phrases everywhere, angry squiggles of "CONTRE LE CPE!" and "NON AU CPE!" Gendarmes prowled in bulletproof gear, crunching broken glass under their boots. Black crepe ribbons hung from the dome of the Pantheon, curling like smoke in the breeze.

Yvonne led us down Rue Saint-Jacques and over the Seine. We approached Notre Dame with jet-lagged awe. Across the plaza, clouds of pigeons startled and circled and landed again among wandering clumps of earthbound tourists. Above us, gargoyles and chimeras leered. The famous flying buttresses looked less airborne and more like claws digging into the earth, petrified tentacles, like the cathedral hadn't been constructed but instead climbed out of the river and beached itself here an eon before anyone felt the first itch to invent a God.

We joined the long line under the Portal of the Last Judgment, the wounded Christ at its center flanked by stone-faced angels praying for our sins. A security guard searched our bags one by one. Inside, Yvonne gestured first to the towering walls of stained glass and their faint purple glow. "If we'd come here a century earlier, before these electric chandeliers, we would've had a better view of what Abbot Suger, an early patron of the Gothic style, called *lux nova*," she said in a loud whisper. "Unlike the walls, which are necessary, of course, but do block the sunlight, the stained glass lets it filter through, transforms it, makes it new, just as Abbot Suger believed God's son Jesus made all things new—the new light."

We followed Yvonne along the outside aisle and looked past the tip of her finger each time she pointed out a Mary, who was everywhere. She wore a crown and held a tiny Jesus on her hip, the Virgin of the Pillar; she knelt at the altar, arms stretched out to Heaven, Jesus dead across her knees, flanked by one Louis, then another. We turned a corner and I looked up to see her again, this time standing alone, looking baffled at the crown of thorns in her hand. The name of the place finally hit me: our lady. Well, somebody's.

It was April and the last time I'd been inside a church was Christmas Eve. Before that, I couldn't remember. Freshman year of college, the first few times I went home for the weekend, my parents and sister and I went to church on Sunday like always. I sat and stood and knelt and stood and sang. The nave was still dark, the acolytes wore the same robes and smocks I'd worn the year before. Everything else was different but here it was just the same. Then it wasn't. While I was away the parish held a fundraiser for new lighting in the nave. The next time I visited, I found myself squinting into an unsettling new brightness. The lacquered wood of the pews and the upturned-ark ceiling all had a harsh new glare, all the wax stains on the aisle runner revealed themselves, and when the priest stepped up to the lectern, tapping his notecards to begin his sermon, confusion flashed through me. Who was this guy? Why was he standing there talking? Why was I sitting here listening? Under the new lights he looked like a regular man in fancy clothes, which of course was all he ever was. When I looked down at my hands in my lap even they seemed wrong—too garish, too obvious.

After that I could only bear Christmas Eve service, when the nave blurred and darkened with candlelight and incense. I told myself it was a matter of decor. I told myself it had nothing to do with what I did or didn't believe. I told myself, like I'd always told myself, that you didn't have to go to church to be a good person, you didn't need to believe anything in particular to be a good person, that being too interested in being a good person was perhaps the wrong way to become one anyway. But I preferred those thoughts blurred and darkened too.

By then, Joe was a student at the Chattanooga outpost of the big state university. When I came up from Atlanta for the weekend, I would spend Friday night at my house with my family and Saturday night at his dorm with him. His roommate was in a months-long one-night-stand with a girl he met at an anti-war rally so we always had the room to ourselves. We'd stay up late fooling around and fall asleep tangled on his narrow bed. We'd sleep late, or he would; often I woke up first and just lay there watching his bedside clock, knowing my parents and sister were getting ready for church, wondering if this was technically the worst thing I would ever do. Often I thought about the WhyKnow lady who taught my eighth grade science class about the horrors of premarital sex. She'd told us all the ways it would ruin our lives; had she detailed its effects on our afterlives, too? Maybe or maybe not but the message came through in a thousand other ways. Now, though, the only thing I felt bad about was that I didn't feel bad.

Now I stood in the nave at Notre Dame, surrounded by virgins, stone and flesh. I made my way to the back and stood watching a line of people approach an altar of flickering votive candles in red glass. One by one they slipped coins into a box, selected a long match, and lit one candle among hundreds. They knelt, crossed themselves, prayed, then rose with tears on their faces. I felt a pang of disorientation, dizzy embarrassment, like I'd sleepwalked into someone else's house.

On the hotel TV that night, the local news showed cars aflame and crowds running from clouds of tear gas in the Latin Quarter. Hundreds of students had marched on the Sorbonne, dozens of thousands all over Paris, half a million across France, all of them unhappy with the government's plans for a young workers' contract. The Gap I'd seen had indeed been on fire, torched by protestors trying to ignite a police van. When I called my parents on my international phone card, mid-afternoon in Tennessee, I waited for them to mention that they'd seen the riots on CNN, waited for any hint of concern in their voices, before assuring them I was safe, perfectly safe. But they didn't say anything so I didn't either.

* * *

The next afternoon the bus carted us across town and deposited us at the foot of Montmartre. "It was here in the year 250 that the man who would become Saint Denis was beheaded by the Roman governors who did not like him converting their people," Yvonne said, shielding her small eyes against the sun. "Despite what you probably think it was not here that he died. No, Saint Denis walked six miles carrying his head in his hands, preaching all the way. Thus the name of this place, Montmartre, mountain of the martyrs. Shall we?" Without waiting for a reply she turned and started up the three hundred stairs to the top.

Above us, the white peaks of the Sacre Coeur rose like meringue from the hilltop. The closer we got the brighter it seemed to glow. Inside the church there was no photography allowed and too many people. I shuffled with everyone into the nave where the only empty space was over our heads. Sunlight filtered in through the stained-glass clerestory windows but everything seemed to give off its own light. Everyone stood staring up at the mosaic of the risen Christ stretching across the concave apse above us. His expression was inscrutable but I was inclined to read some disappointment in his wide-set eyes.

Back in Chattanooga, there was a guy who dressed as

Jesus and dragged a huge wooden cross around town. His dedication had always struck me as obscurely admirable until the day he passed me on the sidewalk while I was sitting at a red light and I noticed his cross had a little wheel on the bottom. That summer, home from college, Marie had encountered him outside a music festival downtown. He handed her a tract she couldn't wait to show me. "Look at this thing," she giggled, pressing it into my hand much like Wheelie Jesus must have pressed it into hers. She was his ideal target, the unsaved heathen, but I was the one whose face flushed as I turned the pages, the words going blurry but the illustrations stark and clear. An airplane crashing into the ocean, a long line of people waiting outside the gates of Heaven, a longer line waiting to descend into a lake of fire. Their bodies were barely bodies, just generic, genderless outlines, no clothes, no fingers or toes, no faces at all. I couldn't get it out of my head. I'd never been enamored with the idea of Heaven, it seemed so lonely to me, but I'd relied upon it anyway. Like a little wheel that made the idea of death easier to drag around. Why did I feel so compelled to kick it aside? What if I was wrong and it was real after all, and Hell too? Marie would be there, if it was, and Joe; even my sister had told me, so offhandedly, "I dunno, I don't really believe in that stuff anymore." How could I believe in something that would consign these people, my best, my most beloved, to an eternity of suffering? How could I believe in something that kept me tethered to that belief by fear alone? In Heaven, perhaps, I wouldn't care who was or wasn't there with me, but if I didn't care then I wouldn't be myself, and not-being myself seemed worse than being nothing.

And yet, nothing was nothing.

Around the time Marie showed me the tract, something strange started happening to me. One day I was driving along a familiar road, right past my old Baskin Robbins, when suddenly something blasted into my mind with such force that my vision went sparkly then dark. I couldn't see and I couldn't breathe. It was a hot black orb and it was howling at me: *You're going to die, you're going to die, you're going to die, you're going to die.* It went on and on and on, and then it was gone, sudden as it came. I could think and see and breathe again and it seemed like no time had passed but it had; I was further down the road, shaking but somehow still driving along. It happened again a few weeks later, back at school, alone in my dorm on a Saturday night. Then again, and again, and again. Years later, I would realize that these were panic attacks; I would learn to brace myself and breathe through them, falling into a wrung-out stupor when they passed. But at the time I just thought of them as visits from the void, previews of my eventual noth-ingness. I couldn't stop them, I thought, anymore than I could make myself believe.

I couldn't do it and I couldn't not do it, not even in the crowded belly of the Sacre Coeur, Jesus looming overhead. I was moved along by the crowd as more and more people pushed into the nave behind us, too many bodies, the air ripe with sour breath, but He didn't seem to mind. His arms were outstretched: nailed to an invisible cross, or flying away, or coming in for a hug. My legs began to wobble and I knew I needed to leave. If I fainted I knew I wouldn't hit the ground—some stranger's body would surely catch me—but I might be mistaken for a true devotee, touched by the spirit, and I couldn't think of anything worse than having to lie, except maybe trying to explain myself.

I pushed my way down the aisle, out the door, out onto the steps, the shining white steps, into the sunlight and the cold air. A busker was playing on the terrace. All the way down the hill, people sat with their backs to the cathedral and their faces toward the city. Somewhere down there, burnt shells of cars were being scraped off cobblestone streets and fresh banners were unfurling from balcony rails. The busker tried to play "The Boxer" but couldn't remember the words so he moved on to "(Everything I Do) I Do It For You" and everyone swayed and sang along.

* * *

In the morning the bus took us southwest from Paris to Chartres in the rain. We could see the cathedral on the horizon miles before we reached the town, gray stone and copper in the fog. Inside, beyond the tall wooden doors, the nave was cool and dark, the gloomy light of day barely filtering through the high-up windows. Jesus stood in the center of a kaleidoscope of scenes from the Last Judgment: the raising of the dead, the weighing of the souls, the blessed ascending to Heaven and the damned falling into Hell.

A service was in progress. It smelled like Christmas. The organ moaned, the altar boys swung their feet, and a priest with a thin white ponytail performed the rites in a language I didn't understand. The congregants sat in rickety chairs arranged in rows over a stone floor inlaid with a labyrinth. There were more of us than them.

"Chartres Cathedral is the fifth and longest-standing structure on this site," Yvonne whispered as she fluffed her damp mane. "Time or fires destroyed all the others and each reconstruction consumed three or four generations of manpower. But pilgrims have been coming here since long before the cathedral was built." She gestured as if to indicate that we were among them. "They came from all over, from far off, and in those days, you know, they did not bathe. You see the floor there—that is where they would sleep. Now the stone is worn down from centuries of

158

washing away their stink." She wrinkled her nose as if she'd been there to smell it herself. Maybe she had.

We followed her down the ambulatory to the mouth of a gated alcove. "Here is what those many pilgrims came to see," she said. "The *sancta camisa*, said to be torn from the tunic Mary wore at the birth of Jesus. It has been spared from every disaster the cathedral has seen since the year 876—fire, war, more fire, more war. It is, some say, a miracle."

I saw tears on some of my classmates' faces as they approached the wrought-iron bars. When they turned and moved away I stepped closer for a better look. What appeared to be a dirty handkerchief was pressed inside a gilded frame, encased in a glass box, and set on a marble pedestal beyond arm's reach. I stood there, staring, waiting to see if I would feel anything. I did not, and then I turned away.

The service continued, out of my sight behind the high stone choir screen that had protected the church's sacred mysteries from the prying eyes of laymen for centuries. I walked along its long curve tracing the scenes from the life of Jesus, bris to ascension. The faces were all gray, eyes blank, heads and hands here and there lost to time. I looked up and there he was on the cross, crown of thorns pressed hard into his head. I turned around and he was a baby again, held tight in his mother's arms. His whole life happening all the time forever.

I felt wobbly again. I found a bench and sat. At the Sacre Coeur it had all been too much but now it was the opposite: a desire for a desire, a yearning against a lack, pulling toward something as it pulled away from me.

I knew the stories in the glass and stone were just the highlights of an old book. I knew the *sancta camisa* was just a lucky scrap.

I knew Jesus was just a man and Mary was just a girl whose son was born and died like all the rest.

I knew that if my head was chopped from my body I wouldn't walk a single step talking about Jesus or anything else.

When I died, I wouldn't float up into the sky, I wouldn't stand in line at the Pearly Gates, I wouldn't get my own white robe and a cloud to spend the rest of forever spying on everyone I loved until they joined me forever too.

And I wouldn't burn for all eternity in a lake of fire.

When I died, I would simply die.

I wanted suddenly and desperately not to know any of this. I wanted not to know better. I wanted to pray and feel like I was talking to anyone other than myself. I wanted to want to walk however far a pilgrim might walk, a hundred miles, a thousand, wanted to want anything as much as a believer wanted God's everlasting love. I wanted to go through all the motions I'd gone through all my life and feel the rightness of them again, or for the first time. I wanted eternity. I wanted what I used to think I already had.

Maybe I would have it again. But I wouldn't find it here.

I stood and walked the length of the nave, past the priest and all the faithful, past my classmates and the pilgrim's worn corner, and pushed my way through one of the tall wooden doors. Outside the rain had stopped and the sun was out but a cold, wet breeze still blew. Down the wide cathedral steps, across a cobblestone plaza, a young woman worked at an easel next to a table with her watercolor paintings laid out for sale. A group of older women were crossing the plaza, scarf-tied heads bent against the wind. I watched them from the doorway, not wanting to go further, not wanting to go back. All at once, a great gust of wind whipped around the cathedral and upturned the easel, which clattered down to the ground as her paintings flew up with a flash of white undersides. At the same time, one of the old women tripped over the curb and tumbled onto the sidewalk. Half the bystanders ran to help the painter and half ran to the fallen woman. Within moments, everything looked as it had before. And I stood by silent, unbelieving, watching the world fall apart and right itself again.

The List

The thing about Nana's second husband was that we all already knew him: Bud was Grandaddy's first cousin, last name also Maddux. He was a widower too, a World War II POW and a woodworker, and he hung around our family functions in an increasingly official capacity in the years after my grandfather died, until he and Nana got married—eloped, actually, after no engagement that I knew of—the summer of 1999, when she was sixty-eight and he was seventy-six. I was fourteen, almost fifteen. A decade later, I would learn that Nana had always felt guilty for how she thought the whole thing must have seemed to my sister and I, strange and hasty if not outright disrespectful to our grandfather's memory. But it had never occurred to me to take offense; if anything, the marriage had come as a relief. It had been too weird for me to think of my *grandmother* having a *boyfriend*; I much preferred her having a *husband*, no matter how he was related to her first one. On this fact, I recall a single bit of commentary from the family at large. "Smart move, Mama," my father's brother Freddy said once, twice, I don't know how many times over the next few years. "You didn't even have to get new checks."

What was more bothersome to me, at the time, was that my grandmother had moved out of the big old white house called Pigeon Roost and into a boring rancher across Cookeville. It only made sense—she needed less space, fewer stairs—but the old house was rented out to some photographer who didn't even redecorate before turning it into their studio. It was strange that families were paying to have a stranger take their portraits in the same rooms where for much of the last century my family had been taking photos of each other for free. It was strange to drive a new route into town, strange to see all of Nana's old stuff rearranged in the new house, and—okay, sure—strange to have Bud's stuff mixed in with hers too. But I'd learned that there were worse things than strange. And also that it was possible, in times of great upheaval, to cling so tightly to remnants of the old world that I could almost make myself forget anything had changed at all. This was easy to do in Cookeville, where my grandmother seemed to have learned the same lesson long ago.

Christmas was a choice remnant and for many years we gripped it by the neck. My parents and sister and I traveled up to Cookeville on December 26 with such unquestioned regularity that when once my mother mentioned we'd made the trip on Christmas Day itself, back when Sarah and I were tiny, I was appalled by even that sliver of deviance, unnerved as always by my life's ability to operate beyond the bounds of my own recollection. But I'm sure that day was much like all the others: rotund tree in the living room, so many presents stacked underneath, Freddy handing them out one by one as everyone else hollered thanks back and forth and discretely pocketed gift receipts, Nana producing a spread of ham and turkey and dressing and big flat green beans and mashed potatoes and sweet potato casserole and biscuits and rolls and three kinds of pie and boiled custard and rum balls that made my father say, "Whoo boy!" and later a general post-festivity slump around the fireplace and/or the television. In montage it would appear something like a commercial for a grocery-store chain or a cholesterol medication. And like the dining room table and the old plaid couch and all the framed photos of long-ago babies, the holiday ritual made the move, largely unscuffed, from the old house to the new. I was a teenager; I was in college; my life became less and less similar to itself. And yet Christmas remained, sentimental and stubborn, like the family that made it so.

* * *

Down in Atlanta, sometimes I imagined holding a string that ran up to Chattanooga and then further up to Cookeville, and at the end of the string was a balloon and I knew one day the balloon would pop. In my mind there was a list: a list of everyone in my family written out in order, oldest to youngest, the order we were supposed to die. I didn't mention this list to anyone—I assumed, perhaps, everyone kept one of their own—though sometimes I would transcribe it to a scrap of paper, in part to reassure myself of its orderliness, in part so I could crush it up and throw it in the trash. On my father's side, Grandaddy and Unk were long ago scratched out; after I pencilled in Bud, Nana was next, but what did that mean? Both of my parents' maternal grandmothers were still alive when I was born, after all, and I'd learned that I was taken along to both of their funerals as an oblivious toddler, which I reminded myself of whenever I felt anxious about all the funerals I'd skipped or skirted around, and all the other inevitable funerals looming in my

165

future. I'd done it before, I told myself, and I could do it again—a half-truth, half-believed, just enough to get by.

In the spring of 2005, toward the end of my second year of college, the list was threatened by an aberration. My mother called me one day to report that my uncle Freddy had fallen off the roof of a cattle trailer and broken his neck. I was not surprised that he had been up on a cattle trailer (he often worked on his wife Susan's father's farm), and I wasn't exactly surprised that he had fallen off (seemed like the first thing I, personally, would do if I stood on a cattle trailer). But I was shocked that he sustained any sort of injury at all. Freddy had always seemed to me a sort of bull-dog, not even a flesh-and-blood dog, more like one of the concrete dogs that denoted the front porch of a University of Georgia fan, which of course I never mentioned to him, he who kept a room in his house dedicated to University of Tennessee paraphernalia. But of course concrete breaks too. At the hospital in Cookeville it was determined that neither his life nor his long-term mobility were in danger, he just needed to be fitted with a halo brace to keep him still and stable while he healed. Not an easy recovery, but a relief to everyone, particularly me and my silently kept list. In order to die, Freddy would have had to skip seven places in line—past Bud and Nana and my mother's two older brothers and both of my parents—and, among so much else, that simply seemed rude.

My parents and sister and I drove up to visit that summer. Freddy and my aunt Susan lived in a small house on some acreage outside Cookeville, and usually when we pulled up the driveway he'd bound out to meet us; after a tour of his massive tomato patch, or visit to the horses someone was always keeping in the back pasture, we'd all sit down together on the porch or in the living room, everyone except Freddy, who might plant one foot up on a chair but otherwise seemed to think he needed to be ready to bound away at a moment's notice. But that day Susan met us at the back door and led us into the living room, where he was propped up in a recliner like a mortified dignitary. The brace caged him: four screws in his skull, each connected to a metal rod that ran down to a thick plastic shoulder brace. Susan had slit the collar of an old Vols T-shirt to fit over the contraption, just barely. Only Freddy's eyes moved, side to side, like someone spying through a painting in a cartoon. When he caught me gawking, he winked. "Oh, this ain't so bad," he said. "You should see the other guy."

He was better by that Christmas, all-important Christmas, moving slow but moving. We ate the lunch Nana made like always, we opened the presents Freddy handed out like always, we sat around afterward in what I thought of as quiet triumph, another point scored against the relentless drag of gravity.

"Too bad you're out of the halo," I said to Freddy. "You could've decorated it real nice for the holidays. Couple ornaments, some tinsel..."

"Yeah, too bad," he said, with less of a laugh than I wanted.

What Freddy knew then—and what the rest of us would be told in the days to come, the news withheld so as not to ruin Christmas—was that he had cancer. He'd gone in for a routine checkup on his neck and, while the once-cracked vertebrae were looking just fine, the doctor had seen some strange spots around them on the scan. Bone spurs, probably, the doctor said, but a test he ordered just in case revealed that they were in fact little tumors, little masses of mutinous cells that would have held onto their own bad news for who knows how long, warping far more than the memory of a December afternoon, if there hadn't been another reason to go poking around. Stupid broken neck saved his life.

* * *

One summer—in retrospect, one of the last summers Nana would live at Pigeon Roost—Sarah and I spent a week in Cookeville, two gangly tweens and our grandmother sweating through the days and nights in the old, un-air-conditioned house. One afternoon, Freddy took us to the swimming pool at the Howard Johnson's, supplying us with a generous quantity of gas-station snacks and not a lick of sunscreen. By the end of the day, I was a bit toasted, but my sister, who had inherited our father and his brother's extremely fair skin but not the childhood on a farm to freckle herself into oblivion, was absolutely scorched. "Hey, Uncle Freddy," she said with a tiny, pained laugh. "I'm like one of your tomatoes." This is what I thought of the first time I saw him after his months-long radiation treatment began. It was spring 2006, Sarah's high school graduation. The skin of his neck was burned raw and oddly pebbled. I couldn't imagine what the inside of his throat looked like. He carried a paper cup with him because he couldn't properly swallow. He sat through the ceremony coughing, grimacing, spitting into the cup. And yet, I was told, his treatment was going well; this evidently immense amount of pain and suffering was somehow the best-case scenario.

What was cancer? What was I supposed to make of it? Grandaddy had been diagnosed and dead in the span of a month (liver). Nana's new husband Bud had it since before they got married (prostate). My father's friend Richard's wife Paula, who I'd stayed with during Unk's funeral and Grandaddy's funeral, had died the previous fall after years of treatment (breast). My mother's brother Frank, Marie's

168

father, once had something excised so swiftly and completely I often forgot all about it (lymphoma?). Cancer, it seemed, guaranteed either quick decline, or protracted suffering, or just a few bad days. You would die now, or you would die later. Maybe it was hell or maybe it was just life itself.

By the Christmas of 2006, a year after his diagnosis, Freddy's treatment was complete. Everything red about him had faded to gray, but his prognosis was good. And in another year's time, his doctors declared the cancer gone. Most of his hair was gone, too, which my father, previously the balder of the two, took every opportunity to gloat about. But Freddy's color had come back, his swagger, his wit. Another year later, Christmas of 2007, while the rest of us drowsed around Nana's living room after lunch, he stood with a foot up on a chair, blocking the muted Fox News on TV, holding court on the subject of baculum. "Y'all know what I mean by baculum, right? I'm talking about penis bones, animal penis bones," he said, digging under his fingernails with a pocketknife blade. He said he knew a man who had a walking stick made out of a bull penis bone. He knew somebody else who had a toothpick custom-carved from a raccoon penis bone. "Come on now, Mama," he said, waggling his knife. "Don't act like you don't know!" Nana squealed, mortified. My sister and I traded looks of panicked delight across the room. Everyone was cackling, crying, hiding their faces, slapping their knees. *He's back!* I kept thinking. How had we almost lost him—twice? Like it was a collective family failing, like we'd all looked the other way for a minute and he wandered off. *Don't you ever do that again,* I wanted to grab his collar and shake him. *You hear me?* As if he was a child, and not the stubbornest man in a long, long line.

Earlier that year, I'd graduated from college; I lived in

Atlanta now and worked at a music magazine where I was an administrative assistant, then an editorial assistant, then an assistant editor. I worked a few shifts a week at a bookstore. At night I ate eggs and beans for dinner and watched the war on TV and called Joe and we talked and talked for hours. He was in college in Chattanooga, and then in grad school in North Carolina, learning how to become a poet. In high school I'd thought college would be when I became myself, and in college I thought after college would be when I became myself, and now I wasn't sure if it would ever happen, or stop happening. When I was in Atlanta, I thought of Chattanooga as home; when I was in Chattanooga, I thought of Atlanta; when I made the long drive up I-85 to visit Joe in his decrepit grad school apartment in Greensboro, I didn't know what to think.

But Cookeville remained itself, as much as any place could: a beloved abstraction, a precious annex, mine and not-quite-mine, just like it had always been. News trickled down to me mostly via my mother, phone calls or e-mails about her and my father's plans to drive up to attend one funeral or another, at which my father often served as a pallbearer. One by one they were dying, all the grownups of indeterminate age and relation who'd come and gone in the background of our visits to Pigeon Roost when I was a kid. They had seemed very old to me then, but now they were *actually* very old, all at the tops of their own grandchildren's lists, if their grandchildren happened to be anything like me. I'd amended my list when Nana married Bud, then again when he died, his slow-moving cancer having become less slow; now she was at the top again, and I hated it, but what could be done? This was, I thought, the order of things.

And so, the spring after that jubilant Christmas, when Freddy went in for a routine checkup and his oncologist saw some strange spots on the scan (always those strange spots on a scan), and the doctor ordered a follow-up, then saw nothing on the follow-up, then ordered a second follow-up, and Freddy refused, saying there was nothing on the scan, they wouldn't see anything on the scan because there was nothing to see, and my father relayed this news to my mother, and my mother relayed it to me—well, I was perversely inclined to believe him. "There's nothing wrong," he was telling everyone. "Don't y'all worry." I always worried, worried like breathing, like my life depended on it—especially that year, 2008, with the economy collapsing and magazines shuttering and my boyfriend accessible only via telephone or a five-hour drive up the most godforsaken stretch of interstate highway in the greater Southeast. To even attempt to not worry was to subvert my very nature. But for Freddy, I was willing. He said it was nothing and so it was nothing. I put it out of my mind. I put it so far out of my mind that in October, when my father said to me, "I talked to Freddy this week—there's something I need to tell you," and then began to cry, I just stared at him, blank and wondering. Whatever could it be? Only the so-called nothing, which of course had been something, and had now been spreading unchecked for months— esophagus, liver, kidneys—so much something there was nothing to be done.

Sarah was off at college in Kentucky and couldn't get home until Thanksgiving. The day after, the four of us drove up to Cookeville together. At the house, Susan met us at the door. In the living room, Freddy was on the couch. He was covered in a thin yellow blanket and he was thin and yellow too. He watched us file into the room. His eyes were wide in his immobile head but this time it wasn't ten pounds of steel holding him still, just his own body. We each bent to give him half a hug. When I put my hands on his shoulders he felt so fragile I thought I might crush him. I grazed the side of his face with a kiss, his skin waxy under silver stubble.

The TV was on, a football game. We arranged ourselves around the living room, my parents each in a recliner, Sarah on a side chair, Susan perched on the arm of the couch. I sat on a footstool pushed against the far wall. Freddy held the remote control, punching at it with thin fingers, flipping from football to basketball and back again. Something resembling a conversation began to lurch around the room but I just stared at the TV, all the bodies scrambling and falling, the whistles, the screams. After a while I felt eyes on me and turned my head. Freddy was lifting one thin hand in my direction, trying to get my attention. He was whispering something, I couldn't tell what. He took a breath and tried again: "Sit in the chair." I realized he was pointing to the rocking chair that sat empty a few feet away from me, closer to the couch, closer to him.

"Oh!" I said. "Oh, I'm fine here."

"Chair," he said again. "More comfortable."

I didn't want to sit in the rocking chair. I wanted the wall to my back and the floor under my feet. I wanted to be on the edge of the room, the edge of my family, the edge of everything. But he was staring at me, and pointing, and dying, so I stood and moved to the rocking chair. It seemed to make him happy. I smiled like I was happy too.

He flipped the channel back to basketball. He fell asleep and woke up and fell asleep again. The rest of us talked around him, I don't remember what about. When it was time to leave we all lined up to kiss him goodbye. Then we clumped around the door pulling on our coats, lingering, delaying. Freddy watched us. "See you at Christmas," he said before we left, and we all said we would, and I knew we were lying.

* * *

Back in Atlanta, where I'd whiled away most of the year in happy denial of the fact that my uncle was very sick, I lived the next few weeks in unshakeable apprehension of his oncoming death. I walked to work, I walked home, I made dinner, I talked to Joe, I slept, I woke again, and all the while I knew, I knew, I knew what I would soon have to know.

What I remember about this time is mostly a sense of being clenched, mentally but also physically bracing for the news to come—maybe by phone call, maybe by thunderclap, or maybe the fact of it would simply appear in my head one afternoon, the arrival of a departure, like the announcement of a broken window by the first stiff breeze through the shattered panes. I thought about it all the time, thought about him all the time, except when I thought of something else, and when I realized I'd been thinking of something else I panicked, as if my mental vigilance had been the one thing sustaining him—as if my aunt and grandmother were doing nothing at his bedside in Cookeville, as if my father wasn't splitting himself in two to be with them when he didn't have to be at work in Chattanooga—as if such a thing might be possible at all. But I did try, and the trying made me sadder still, because the longer I held him there, the more I realized I wasn't even sure who I was holding. I had never really considered him as a person before, as someone who existed beyond my specific claim to him. I didn't know, for instance, the sort of things I learned, often with zero effort, about people I met in Atlanta: what his job was, what he studied in college, if he even graduated from college. I lacked the basic trivia and I lacked the answers to the questions I hadn't even thought of asking yet, which I maybe wouldn't have asked even if I had the chance. But I was twenty-four and he was fifty-two. I thought I should at least have the chance.

In late December, I drove up to Chattanooga for the holidays with a duffel bag of dark pants and sweaters. "Just in case," my mother had suggested—remembering, I'm sure, my hissy fit before Joe's grandmother's visitation years ago: *But I don't have anything black to wear!* I arrived at my parents' house just as my father was leaving again for Cookeville. "I'll be home again tomorrow," he said as he kissed my forehead in the doorway. In the morning he called to say he'd be back the next day; the next day he called to say he didn't know when he'd be back. That night, my mother and sister and I were wrapping presents in our own corners of the house when the phone rang. I was in the kitchen and the cordless was sitting right there next to me but I didn't touch it. Instead my mother walked in, picked it up, said "Hello?" as she crossed through the dining room, went silent in the living room, then stopped in the front hall, parquet creaking under her feet. "Okay," she said after a while. "Okay."

Later, I would realize that I knew nothing about the night he died except that he died. I could manage to imagine only bodies bent over in a dark room—his mother, his brother, his wife—his own body hidden from me by my own mind. Perhaps I could have asked. But to ask, I would have to want to know.

That was Sunday. Christmas was Thursday. Hooper-Huddleston, good old Hooper-Huddleston, suggested Wednesday for the burial but nobody wanted a funeral on Christmas Eve. Nobody wanted to wait a week, either. So it would be visitation on Monday night, burial Tuesday morning.

Nobody wanted that either, really. Nobody wanted any of it.

It was raining when we pulled up to the funeral home late Monday afternoon, night already creeping in, the day after the shortest day of the year. A Hooper-Huddleston man held open the door for us, Nana and my aunt Susan and my father and mother and Sarah and I, miserable guests of honor. I'd hoped for a labyrinth of foyers like at Joe's grandmother's visitation but instead we walked right into the too-bright reception hall where a dozen rows of red-padded chairs were all that separated us from the casket at the far end of the room. The bottom half was closed and covered in evergreen boughs. The top half was open. Another Hooper-Huddleston man stood there squinting and dabbing at my uncle's face with a little sponge. Bottles and brushes were arrayed on the seat of a chair nearby. He looked up, saw us, packed his kit and hurried away. The first Hooper-Huddleston man herded us down the middle aisle. Up close, Freddy's face was all wrong: sunken but puffy, skin chalky and greenish under the fluorescent lights. He was wearing makeup, but stranger still, he was wearing a suit. Once I might have said he wouldn't be caught dead in a suit. But here we were.

People began to arrive and didn't stop arriving for hours. At first they came in the door and came down the aisle and walked right up to my aunt, who stood like a small guardian by the casket, and then a line began to form. It ran the length of the aisle, through the foyer, out the door and into the wet, brittle night. The room smelled like lilies—there were lilies everywhere—and the lilies stank, and the building's heat kept blasting on to offset the continual draft of the forever-opening door, and the people kept coming. One after another the people at the front of the line stepped up to the casket and took Susan's hands in their own or folded her into a long, shaking hug, and then she stood there as they stepped closer to look at Freddy in the casket, and sometimes they covered their faces with their hands, they cried and she cried and they said things to her that I couldn't hear and she just nodded, like all of it was true. When they turned away from him, away from her, they turned toward my grandmother, who was sitting in the front row, and they cried with her too, and they came along and cried with my father, who stood with my sister and mother and I off to the side, though by then the people often seemed tired of crying, and of course some of them never cried at all, I realized when I began to see them up close and one-by-one. The high-school buddies and the old basketball teammates and the fourth cousins and the neighbors, the dentist, the man who rented Unk's old house. Some seemed dazed, shaking their heads, others as blank as they might be at the DMV. Some said that they hadn't even known Freddy was sick, some confessed they had known but hadn't really believed it, some seemed not even to believe it now.

Hours passed, hours and hours. I stood and I sat. I ate dry sandwiches from a plastic tray. I watched my grandmother, who I did not want to die, and I thought, *But you were supposed to be next.* She knew this, of course. She knew it was all wrong. That afternoon she'd stood blank-faced in her kitchen telling us she couldn't stop thinking about how when Freddy was a baby she'd sometimes rock him to sleep while smoking a cigarette. "I just wonder," she said. "I just wonder." She couldn't say it but we all knew what she meant and we all told her no, no, no, of course not, but I don't think she believed us. Now she sat there, ten feet of thin carpet between her and the casket. Sometimes she sat with her whole body turned away from it, leaning into a conversation with someone, carrying on like she was anywhere else. Sometimes she sat facing forward, staring at him, or at least the box of him, like the rest of the world had slipped away and it was just the two of them, the way it started.

I watched my father, the way he moved through the room, shaking the hands, accepting the hugs, absorbing or deflecting everyone else's sadness, and I realized he must have done the same thing at after Grandaddy died, and Unk, and he would do the same when Nana died too. Because this is what you were supposed to do, and my father always did what you were supposed to do, and he had taught me to do this too, and so one day I would have to bury him, and one day I would have to bury my mother, or my sister. Unless they had to bury me.

I watched my aunt, still standing at the casket, the night and the line of people nearly at its end. She'd been twenty-two when she married Freddy twenty-five years earlier. A year more than my whole life. It seemed like so much time and nowhere close to enough. Sunday night, I'd called Joe to tell him that Freddy had died and I was going with my family up to Cookeville for a few days. "Do you want me to come with you?" he said. "I will come with you." But I'd said no. We'd been together six years by then, and he'd met my father's family plenty of times, but I still thought of them as occupying two distinct spheres of existence and I was too daunted by the prospect of reconciling them in the midst of everything else. Or I had been. Now I remembered sitting with him in the hallway at his grandmother's visitation, the weight of our hands together, and I knew that comfort would only grow in proportion to any sadness I could ever feel. I wanted to run—to escape this room of death, to be anywhere else, but mostly to get myself back to him. I realized, with a sick flash, that my keys were in my bag, my car was in the parking lot. A small part of me thought, *Go*. A bigger part of me thought, *No, stay. But remember this. You want him here. You will always want him here.*

* * *

When we left that night, used Kleenex covered the floor like damp snow. The next day, all the dirty tissues were gone but the coffin was still there, and even more of the awful lilies. A man played a long, sad song on an electric keyboard. My family took our seats up front. Behind us, the room filled in—a smaller crowd than the night before, but still so many people. This one thing, at least, felt right.

Up by the casket there was a lectern and soon a man appeared behind it and began to speak. The man was a pastor of some kind and he seemed to think that he knew my uncle but I wasn't sure. He seemed not to know about all the Christmases, or the sunburn at the Howard Johnson's —certainly not the monologue about the animal penis bones —or the dozens, hundreds, of other stories that anyone who knew him even a little bit would have had to sift through to speak of his life. The man didn't seem to understand, had perhaps not personally experienced, how the whole balance of a room could shift, could right itself, when Freddy walked into it. The man was talking only about some generic person, a Son and a Brother and a Husband, a stick figure. The man did seem aware that Freddy loved football and grew tomatoes but that only made me angrier. *How dare he! Who told him? How dare they!*

After a while the man said, "And now I want to call up the family." He stepped back from the lectern and stretched his arms out wide, waggling his fingers to draw us near. We all stood—my aunt and my grandmother and my father and mother and Sarah and I, and Susan's sister and her husband and son and wife and baby, and who knows how many

178

cousins, half the room probably, another sign this man knew not of whom he spoke or he would have just said, "All y'all please stand." The man drew us all to him, best he could. "Let us pray," he said. We all bowed our heads and he called up to God on our behalf, begging for His peace and healing and to bless us and show us His wisdom in all our pain. I could hear all the capital H's. I could hear the echo of a man in a long-ago gray room: *If you died today, do you know if you'd go to Heaven?* All along I'd been crying, everyone was crying, pink-faced and mostly dignified, but now we were wailing, sobbing, gasping, clutching at one another. I was no longer supporting my own weight, I was held upright by the crush of bodies around me. The man went on and on and my head kept popping up above the fray, desperate for air. When I did I could see the man standing over us, above us somehow, his own head tilted back, eyes shut. *How dare he. How dare he. How dare he.* Behind him my uncle lay in his box, still dead.

And then we were all out in the parking lot, a line of black cars waiting in the flat gray afternoon. The pallbearers loaded the casket into the first hearse. A Hooper-Huddleston man steered my aunt Susan toward the second car then beckoned for my sister and I to follow. "Family this-a-way," he said, and I turned to see my parents and Nana disappearing into the third car. It was all out of order, wasn't it? But I was tired and cold and the man's hand was firm on my back. We got in and the driver came around with an overflowing armful of green velour blankets and tucked them around our laps. I felt like a sickly child. I felt for the first time in so long like I thought I should feel.

We drove to the cemetery, a long line of cars with little funeral flags flying. It was raining, still raining. The cemetery was on a hill behind a tiny white church. The cars parked and the people emerged and moved up the gravel driveway on foot. A green Hooper-Huddleston tent marked the spot. It stood over a deep, precise, rectangular hole, next to which a half-moon of folding chairs teetered on a strip of muddy AstroTurf. All these small things I never thought to imagine all the times I tried to picture Grandaddy's funeral. My grandmother and my aunt and my mother and my sister sat in the chairs. Someone nudged me toward them but my knees wouldn't bend. I stood behind them, next to my father.

The pallbearers picked their way across the gravel and onto the slick grass with the coffin gripped between them. I watched them watch their feet. I watched one of the men glance up for a second and his eyes flashed open wide. I looked over my shoulder to see what he saw: the crowd cascading all the way up the hillside, everyone huddling under umbrellas among the gravestones. The pallbearers set the casket down onto a metal brace that framed the hole. The pastor man reappeared and said some words I couldn't hear. Then the metal brace issued a mechanical groan and the box began its descent into the earth. When the thing clanged to a stop, two men in dirty pants took away the frame and began shoveling dirt back into the hole. And somehow that was that.

Everyone began talking again at the same time. Startled, I turned to say something to my father but he had already turned to say something to somebody else. Everyone was saying hello, shaking hands. Something had broken, something had lifted. Someone was wearing an orange necktie printed with hedgehogs. Someone else was laughing. I was laughing. Along the edge of the cemetery, up and down the hill, the chain link fence caught flower arrangements blown from their graves, like the ones that would collect in the ditch along the cemetery across from my elementary school playground. I'd tried so hard not to look but I could remember the flutter of their faded silk petals in the wind. Not real, exactly, but almost alive.

It was nearly dark when the Hooper-Huddleston cars got us back to town, trees bare and black against a weird tarp-blue sky. The day after the shortest day of the year. We drove our own cars to another tiny white church. From the parking lot, the parish hall windows glowed. Inside I could see folding tables laid with casseroles, platters of little sandwiches, piles of sliced country ham, biscuits, pimento cheese, bowls of pale winter fruit. People were already moving down the buffet, filling their plates, talking, laughing. Through one window I saw Susan, then caught myself looking for Freddy. I wondered if this was the hard part, actually, whatever came next.

I stopped on the church's front steps. At the house next door, lights were flickering on: white lights, rainbow lights, red and green and blue strung along every eave and wrapped in tight spirals around all the bushes. It was a meticulous display. What looked like empty trash bags lay across the yard. Then a hum filled the air and the bags began to grow, limp and deformed at first, their true shapes slowly becoming clear. A snowman, a penguin, a giant Santa Claus. Like new ghosts they rose from the ground, invertebrate, arms full, welcoming the sky.

Uncertain Wing

On the last night of 2008, Joe and I went to a New Year's party where I drank too much three-dollar wine, yelled at him for making fun of the bands on *Dick Clark's Rockin' Eve*, and passed out on our friends' futon moments after the ball dropped. The next day we drove in my Subaru back to Atlanta, him quiet behind the wheel, me woozy in the passenger seat, ashamed of how mean I'd been to him the night before, especially because I agreed with him—the guy from Daughtry *did* sound like he was straining to pass a massive turd. An apology occasionally tried to burble up in my throat but never quite made its way out.

Inside my apartment, the air was cold and stale. I hadn't been home since before Christmas, since before my uncle died. But now here we were, and it was time for dinner. Joe opened and quickly closed the refrigerator. The cabinets were empty too. "I'll go to Kroger," he said. "Spaghetti?" I grunted and he tossed his car keys to himself. "Be right back."

When the door closed behind him I was alone for the first time in weeks. I sat down on the bed and listened to his footsteps taper off down the hallway and when I couldn't hear them anymore I realized that he was going to die. Not someday, not far off in the future, but today, that night, in just a matter of minutes. I felt certain of this in a way I hadn't felt certain about anything in a very long time. Joe was going to the grocery store and he was going to die and there was nothing, absolutely nothing, that I could do to stop it. I could only follow him with my mind: He was down the back staircase, crossing the parking lot, starting up his car. I looked at the clock. What time had he left? I hadn't noticed. God, I was stupid. I stood up from the bed and sat on the loveseat. I stood up from the loveseat and stared at myself in the mirror. Stupid, stupid. I watched the clock. He was parking now, he was walking through the sliding doors, he was getting a basket—he always got a basket, he never got a cart, even when he had too much for a basket—infuriating. He was going up and down the aisles, he was waiting in the checkout line. He was back in the parking lot, back in the car, driving toward home, my home, whatever this place was to him. I opened my blinds and stood by the windows. It was not late but it was dark. The first day of the year had turned into the first night of the year and the cars went up and down the street, the buses went up and down the street, red lights one way, white the other. I wondered if I would be able to see the crash as it happened. I would certainly be able to hear it. All the leaves off the trees, sound traveling strange in the cold air. The pickup truck barreling through the intersection, the carjacked SUV, the cyclist skidding out in the curve. I thought of calling ahead to 911: *Look, please, you've got to believe me!* What was the last thing I said to him? I had a sinking feeling that it was something like, "Later, tater." If I'd known what I knew a minute earlier, I could have at least said I love you. Or, god, duh, I could have warned him, kept him back, kept him safe. *Look, please—*

Then I heard it. Not a crash, not a siren—knuckles against a door. When I opened up he said, "Honey, I'm home!" like a sitcom dad. I followed him to the kitchen which was too small for both of us so I stood in the narrow doorway watching him unload the bags. He hummed to himself, some aimless tune. He stopped when he realized I was crying, at which point I realized I was crying. "Oh my god, what's wrong?" he said, dropping the mushrooms and wrapping his arms around me.

"I thought you were going to die out there," I said.

"Oh," he said. "Well, see, I didn't."

"But how could I know you wouldn't?" I spluttered into his neck. His skin was so soft there and he smelled like himself, like he always had, like he always would until he actually died, whenever that would be. "How could I know you were coming back?"

"Because I'm always going to come back," he said. "Anytime I leave, I'm always coming back."

Why were people always saying things like that? I'm coming back, talk to you later, see you at Christmas. The infuriating certainty, the arrogance of all these promises just begging to be broken.

* * *

I'd moved into the apartment in May 2007, the day after I graduated from college. It was a studio in an old building, hardwood floors and glass doorknobs, three tall windows facing an elementary school across the street. For the first couple weeks my alarm clock was the crossing guard's whistle. I stood at the window and drank my coffee watching the little kids and their too-big backpacks walking in for the day.

And then one morning, silence. Summer break had come, but—for the first time—not for me.

I spent my days at the magazine office, some evenings at the bookstore, and, excepting Joe's weekend visits, every night alone. Occasionally, I remembered with a jolt that I lived here now, in Atlanta, or technically a little town called Decatur that the bigger city of Atlanta was eating up like a dot in the Pac-Man maze. College had offered some plausible deniability, but now I paid rent, paid bills, registered to vote, got a library card, all in a place that for years had seemed to me like barely a place at all. Atlanta was where we went for year-end field trips in elementary school, where my family sat in traffic jams on our way to or from the beach—somewhere to exist only temporarily. The city had always struck me as having no sense of itself, no edges and no center. Now here I was, and I was beginning to feel centerless too.

For as long as I could remember, I'd always felt a little sad in the summertime, especially in July, that uncanny apogee, the furthest I ever got from the reassuring confines of the school calendar, which for seventeen years had given structure and meaning to my life. Usually the promise of fall semester was enough to pull me through the summer slump. But that year, when the crossing guard came back, and the kids and their backpacks, my days stayed the same. At the magazine, I was still learning to live at the mercy of the editorial calendar, marking time with pitch meetings and traffic meetings, rounds of proofs and copy edits and fact-checks, the late-night high-wire act of closing each issue, perilous every time like it was the first time. I loved the work, but there was a sense of precariousness that I never could shake, a suspicion that landing this dream job right out of college must be too good to be true (what was the catch?), fueled by an increasing awareness of the dire economic realities of publishing a print music magazine in the mid-2000s (this was the catch). And anyway, I was in the office by nine-thirty and home by six, no homework, no roommates, nobody's immediate needs to fulfill except my own, and half the time I wasn't even sure what those might be. What was I supposed to do with all of this *time*? It was August, September, October, but that old July feeling lingered. My days fell into weeks and the weeks into months and when I looked up and out I could see years spilling out before me like so many reams of blank ledger paper, long and white and crisp, a sight I thought should fill my heart with sparks of optimism and ambition, but which instead overpowered me with dread. More and more I felt dogged by an eerie non-feeling, a sense of deep darkness that got deeper and darker the more I tried to push it away. I began to cry a lot—never at work, only at home, and so regularly that it came to seem like just another one of my body's excretory functions. "I don't know *why* I'm crying," I sobbed to Joe on the phone one night. "Things are good, really good! I'm happy! I should be happy. Why am I not happy?"

"I think you might be depressed," he said.

"Jesus, I'm not *depressed*," I wailed back. "I'm just really sad, like, all of the time."

By then I'd Googled "depression symptoms" more than a few times and decided that this couldn't possibly be my problem. One of the common symptoms was "difficulty sleeping," but for me sleep remained life's one reliable mercy. Most nights I could count on eight to ten hours of perfect, steady slumber. I loved sleep. I loved how I always knew exactly what to do, how it freed me from my stupid brain and the stupid crush of time, how easy it felt there on the flip-side of consciousness. I loved it so much that I began to worry I secretly wanted to kill myself. Sometimes I even asked myself, just to check, "Do I want to kill myself?" The answer was always no. I did not want to die. But for the first time in my life I didn't entirely dread the thought of it. For the first time in my life, when I thought about death, I didn't feel anything at all. In this way it was like everything else.

One night I dreamed of a pale white flashing light and then I woke up and the dream was real, a strained glow was stuttering into the dark of my apartment from somewhere beyond the blinds. I dragged myself to the window, peered between two plastic slats, and saw it was coming from the elementary school across the street. The building's alarm system was firing, lights flashing in each one of its big-windowed classrooms. I could hear the sirens bleating down the hallways, echoed and muffled by the walls and the distance. Some fire trucks came howling down the block. Firemen stomped into the school and disabled the alarm. There was no fire. They returned to their trucks and rumbled back into the night, and the school sat dark and silent again. It stared at me. I stared back. The alarm still rang in my brain, muffled but insistent, unable to be convinced that all was well.

Some weekends I drove up to visit Joe in Greensboro. We would drink with his MFA classmates or stay in and watch *Mystery Science Theater* 3000 and the next day soothe our hangovers with huevos rancheros at a Mexican restaurant called Mexico Restaurant. I liked being anywhere with him, even his apartment where on move-in day he'd had to clean the previous tenant's dried vomit out of the kitchen sink. But sometimes I would wake up and stare at the cracked ceiling over his double-stacked air mattresses and my brain would pulse with its alarm. What was happening, what was going to happen? I didn't know the answer so I knew it was something bad. Was I going to lose my job? Would I have to leave Atlanta, would I have to move back in with my parents, would I move in here with

Joe? Where would I work? I'd heard of being a copywriter; could I be a copywriter? What even was a copywriter? I would cry then, like I'd cried on the drive up, like I'd cry on the drive back home. Some other weekends I went to weddings, sometimes with Joe and sometimes alone, and I cried at the weddings too, even when the ceremonies were suffocatingly religious, even when the whole relationship was bad news. These tears in particular mystified and embarrassed me. For all the romantic longing that consumed my teenage years, I'd never felt especially compelled toward marriage, and the prospect actually held less interest after I met Joe; we were in love, we were 2gether4ever, but when I tried to imagine getting married to him, I pictured two little kids stumbling around in dress-up clothes—adorable but unserious. And then by the time we were what I thought of as "old enough," we felt so inoperable without each other, despite the distance, that the idea of marriage seemed almost redundant. And yet I craved the redundancy. And yet I balked at my craving. Was marriage a door, one if I pushed through would lead me into the rest of my life? Or was it a domino, and pushing it would set off an unstoppable chain reaction, tiles falling fast and hard beyond my control all the way down the road to death?

It was 2007, it was 2008, it was 2009. My uncle died, the bookstore cut my hours and then closed, I wrote my first cover story for the magazine and it almost didn't get printed because we almost ran out of money but then we didn't, and in response to all of these things, and many lesser things, the muffled alarm kept ringing in my head. In college, I'd had my visits from the hot black orb and its hectoring reminders of my ultimate nothingness, but this was something new— not so nasty, but harder to shake.

Nothing seemed to help, but taking walks didn't make it worse. I walked all around my neighborhood, up and down the hills and around the looping side streets. I saw the bungalows and the colonials and the tudors, I saw the couples doing yard work and the kids playing basketball and dogs running up and down fence lines. (Dogs. Dogs! Didn't they know they were going to die?) I liked walking right at dusk, after everyone went in for dinner but before they closed their blinds. I liked seeing them in there, glowing against the growing darkness, all the little lives; maybe one day I would have one too. I walked and walked. I could walk for hours. Then even this turned against me. Thirty minutes, twenty, ten. If I stayed out for too long the alarm in my head got louder, turned into something else: shallow breath, pressure in my throat. I would have to turn home immediately and sit with the lights off until I could breathe again.

One night I left my apartment, walked to the corner, then stopped. The street was empty except for a man and a woman and a dog a few houses down. When I saw them, some kind of invisible hand tightened around my neck. I turned and ran home. Back upstairs, I shook and cried and cried like I'd actually been mugged. Then I lay there quiet for a long time. Then my phone rang. I answered and my mother said, "Are you okay?"

"Oh yeah, I'm fine," I said, trying to sniffle casually. "Maybe just getting a cold."

She called the next night too. By then I hadn't left my apartment all day and I was wondering if I ever would. "Are you okay?" she asked again.

"No," I said, and this time I told her everything.

"Look, sweet girl," she said when I ran out of steam. "I can't tell you what to do. But I think you need to go to the doctor. Tell him what you told me. Tell him exactly how you've been feeling."

"But," I said, feeling the need to protest but not sure what or why, an old habit.

"They make medicine for this," she said. Was she laughing? "Believe me, once it kicks in, you'll regret not doing it sooner." She was definitely laughing. "At least I did."

A memory floated to the surface of my septic-tank mind. One weekend, home from college freshman year, I'd sat down at the old Compaq Presario just after my mother stood up. When I opened Internet Explorer I saw the tab of recently visited websites. At the top of the list (of course I clicked) was an American Psychological Association webpage about depression symptoms. I wondered who in the world she'd been looking them up for. Surely not herself! My mother wasn't depressed, she just seemed sad sometimes, and other times she seemed to be carrying around something heavy I couldn't see, and she could be edgy and easily rankled, and she'd always been that way, on and off, for as long as I could remember. But that was just her, wasn't it? Just like it was just me?

I dreaded calling to make the appointment so thoroughly that I was still dreading it when I sat on the exam table a few weeks later and the doctor said, "What brings you in today?" I told him everything very quickly so he wouldn't have a chance to interrupt and tell me I was wrong. When I was done, he sighed and looked down at his shoes. He looked at them for a long time, then looked up, past me, past the ceiling. He had a long, lumpy face.

"I joined the Navy when I was seventeen," he said at last. "And there were these guys—big guys. Muscles, tattoos, hard drinkers. They were always going after the girls, they always got the girls. And they were always having more fun than anybody else. More fun than me, for sure. I wasn't having any fun. But the big boys, they knew how to have fun. I tried to keep up. I wanted to be one of them.

One of the big boys. I couldn't drink more than three beers without puking. I puked most nights. Miserable. I stopped short of tattoos. I was worried about diseases."

My legs dangled off the side of the table. I swung them like a child. I did not know what to say.

"Our type," he said, gesturing between us. "We need to know what's going on today, what's going on tomorrow, what's going on next month, next year, five years from now." He paused again and looked right at me. I tried to imagine him young. I tried to imagine him puking. After a few seconds he shrugged and shook his head, like he was coming out of a daze. "Citalopram, ten milligrams, once a day," he said, scribbling on a pad. "Just stop at the vampires on your way out."

I made my sacrifice to the phlebotomists then drove to CVS. The pills were tiny orange things that rattled in the orange bottle like cupcake sprinkles. I swallowed one that night, then stared at myself in the mirror.

"Okay," I said.

A few days later, a nurse called from the doctor's office. She said my bloodwork came back and my thyroid levels were high. "Hypothyroidism has been known to cause anxiety," she said. "That's probably not helping you any."

"Oh yeah," my mother said when I told her. "I have that too. Sorry, babe."

I drove to CVS again to pick up my levothyroxine. Now it was green pills in the morning, orange pills at night, and a new tone to the alarm ringing in my head. What would these things do to me? Who would I be when they started working? Who was I now, anyway? Was I erasing myself? Or what if nothing changed? What if I was unfixable—too chronically, terminally myself?

Then a few days later I was walking home from work when suddenly my head felt quiet. My legs felt stronger, my whole body lighter. It was late July and the sidewalk was hot and solid under my feet. I was walking, walking and feeling, feeling and breathing, a real person in a real place after all, a little town in a city in a state in a country in the world, a world I was returning to like a long-closed apartment, strange and familiar all at once.

* * *

Labor Day weekend, I went up to see Joe in Greensboro. All my old questions remained, but now I didn't care as much that I didn't know the answers. My last night in town, I drove us up to a restaurant that was supposed to have incredible views of the mountains. When we got there all the outside tables were taken so we sat in the dark dining room where all we could see was each other. I drank one beer and got sleepy. I could never hang with the big boys, either. In the parking lot after, I tossed Joe my keys to drive us home.

"Man, I just ate so many beans," he said as he started the car. "I got that burrito, which was full of beans, and then I don't know why but I ordered beans on the side too—I mean, did you see all those beans?"

"I saw," I said. "It did seem like a lot of beans."

"It was some serious beanage. I'm on the express train to Fartsville."

We drove along for a while and every so often he would roll down his window with a guilty glance in my direction. He made one turn, then another. I had no idea where we were but I didn't care. We were together and headed, however circuitously, toward our temporary home. He turned down a long, empty road stretching between two steep embankments, their cascades of kudzu glowing green in the streetlights, the distance between them occasionally

193

spanned by a railroad bridge or a two-lane overpass. I wondered what was up and over there, just out of sight.

As we approached one overpass, something about it caught my attention. I could just barely make out a silhouette of someone leaning against the railing, hunched as if peering down at the street below. And just as we were about to drive under, I saw something moving quickly downwards, toward us, a dark shape that for a strange, stretched second hovered right in front of us, a hole punched in the night.

The sound was like nothing I'd heard before: a brutal metallic *POCK!* It happened and it kept happening, the echo, the aftershock, ringing down into my molars. Joe stomped on the brakes and said, "WHAT THE FUCK." The car skidded cockeyed across two lanes, the overpass now in our rearview. "WHAT THE FUCK," he said again.

"A rock," I heard myself saying. "Someone dropped a rock."

Joe stared at me, his face white in the streetlight glow. My hand went to my forehead, expecting to feel blood and dented skull, brain pulsing under my fingers. But it just felt like my head. I looked down, expecting to see my lap full of shattered glass. But there was no glass. I looked up at the windshield: smooth and intact.

"We're okay," Joe said, or maybe I said it, then one of us said, "Let's go home, let's just go home."

At Joe's apartment, he parked and we walked inside quickly, not looking back, not ready to see the damage. In the light of the morning, when we carried my bags to the car, we surveyed it: On the passenger side, a few inches above the top edge of the windshield, there was a cluster of dents, each four or five inches long, the biggest a half-inch deep with two sharp, distinct gouges down the middle. The paint was shorn away and the raw metal showed through. Joe ran his hand over them and I felt along my forehead again, my hairline, my soft thudding temple. A few inches lower, a few seconds earlier, a few fractions of whatever—what was the difference between life and death? And what had it been, anyway? I said a rock but maybe it was a brick or a cinder block or a cracked-off corner of a street curb? A meteorite. A baker's palm sinking into dough, warm and easy. The green pill and the orange pill hummed in my blood, tamping down the panic that a few months earlier might have crushed my brain in its own way. All this fear, all this bracing for disaster, what did it even matter? I'd seen it coming and I hadn't even seen it coming.

What else couldn't I see? So much, so much, like always. In May, Joe would be done with his program. He would consider going out on the academic job market, becoming a writing professor like all of his writing professors before him; he would tell me, "It's kind of like the Army, you go wherever they need you," but I needed him too, but I wouldn't say this, but he knew. That spring I would move out of my studio and into a one-bedroom apartment down the street and he would arrive one night and in the morning he was still there and every morning he was still there. That summer, he would get a job as a copywriter. Two weeks later, I would lose my job at the magazine when a last-ditch deal to shore up its finances fell through. I would eventually become a copywriter too, but first I would get a job at a candy store. In December, I would come home one night, sugar-glazed from the holiday frenzy, and he would hold out a little box and ask me if I wanted to get married, and I did, of course I did. The next August, on an afternoon so muggy you could cut the air like cake, we'd say some words back and forth and our friends would read Emily Dickinson and Walt Whitman, and we would eat barbecue and dance in a barn, and at the end of the night young Rod Stewart would sing "Ooh La La," and I too would wish that I knew all I know now when I was younger. What was happening? What was going to happen? We didn't know. We never did. But we were married now in the eyes of the State of Tennessee and some alleged god and everyone we loved, and it was a domino and it was a door, and we were pushing through, we were falling, together.

But first we had to stand there behind his apartment in Greensboro, staring at those dents in the roof of my car, thinking not about what had happened, not what might happen, but what might have been. We had to stand there for a long time, until I had to leave, and Joe wrapped his arms around me. "Drive safe," he said, and all we could do was laugh.

Four Dogs

Sadie was an orange-and-white Brittany Spaniel, soft ears, stub tail, a runaway hunting dog, probably, who screamed at the neighborhood fireworks every Fourth of July. The first time I saw her she was splayed on her back in a patch of sun on the concrete floor of the outdoor kennel at the city animal shelter, and I thought she was dead. I was ten, halfway to eleven. A few weeks earlier, my parents had called Sarah and I downstairs one afternoon, saying they had something important to tell us, and their tone was so serious, and my memories of Grandaddy dying and Unk dying were still so fresh, that I began to cry, wondering who it might be this time. But nobody was dead —"Oh no, honey!"—quite the opposite: "We think you girls are old enough now," my father began, and my mother continued, "To help take care of a dog!" And then Sarah started crying because she was so happy, and I just never stopped, the dredges of my dread flushed out by new joy. And now I misunderstood again: I saw the dog, the dead dog, white and pink belly turned up to the sun, flies buzzing around, and I almost turned to run, but then she wriggled back to life, resurrected by our presence, leapt to her feet and began flinging herself at the metal gate, pink tongue flapping out of a pink mouth, ecstatic at our arrival. She continued to greet us this way for almost the rest of her life.

At home, my father fenced in a quadrant of our backyard and installed a Dogloo lined with cedar shavings and a plywood lean-to under which we set a water bowl and a food bowl. It did not seem strange at the time for a dog to live her whole life outside, at least not this dog. Sadie spent most of her days sitting on the roof of her lean-to, a three-foot height she could easily clear, which gave her a view of cars going up and down the street and anyone who pulled into our driveway and anyone who came out the side door into the yard. When she saw someone coming, she would launch herself off the roof and crowd the gate, leaping and wiggling and howling; my parents were tall enough to gently shove her down, but Sarah and I were routinely overpowered, pinned to the fence as the dog maniacally slurped our faces and scrabbled at us with her dirty paws, laughing at first and then crying and then screaming until someone came and freed us from her chaotic affections. A few times she pounced before we could close the gate, then pushed it wide and made a break for it: out of the pen, across the yard, an orange streak disappearing up the street faster than any of us could hope to follow. She would lap the subdivision a few times then trot home, panting through a maniac grin. My father was the only one who could keep up with her on a walk, and even then she strained against the leash, wheezing, eyes bugging, no distance ever enough. All of these factors combined to complicate the original plan for my sister and I to actively participate in the dog's care and keeping. Also it was raining sometimes, and dark sometimes, and very cold or very hot sometimes, and we loved her, but we were children. We provided her with affection, when the weather and our attention spans allowed. Our mother did the rest.

By the time I went off to college, Sadie had settled into middle-age, still insatiable on her walks but more inclined to laze around like she'd been doing the first time I saw her, occasionally even inside the house. Not seeing her every day meant I tracked her aging differently, was sometimes startled by it on my trips home: how the orange of her face became more and more white, how her eyes began to cloud, how her once-wiry form grew more and more stout. And then there were her farts: silent, noxious, room-clearing. I blamed the vole brains, personally, but the veterinarian said canine diabetes. My mother began buying insulin at cost and administering injections at strict twelve-hour intervals, six o'clock in the morning and six o'clock at night. It worked for a while. But by the time I moved home the summer between my junior and senior years, the dog couldn't be left alone in her pen during the day because she was afraid of her water bowl and would too quickly get dehydrated, and she couldn't be left alone in the house because she would get lost in familiar rooms and pee everywhere, and she couldn't be left outside overnight because she would just yowl and yowl and yowl, and so she and my mother slept together in the living room, my mother on the couch and the dog on the floor on a pile of blankets that she would soak with pee by morning.

That summer, the last I would live at home, I often slept late enough that my mother had already washed and dried and replaced the dog's blanket bed by the time I shuffled downstairs. But still I knew it was untenable. But still I was confused the night my mother said to me, "So I talked to the vet today."

I said, "About what?"

"Well, about Sadie."

"About *what* about Sadie?" Now I was just being petulant. I wanted her to say it out loud—wanted to make her pretend, like I was pretending, that I didn't know exactly what she was talking about.

"About putting her to sleep," she said finally, exasperated. "She's not getting better. She'll only get more sick from here. She's suffering. And, you know, I'm suffering. She doesn't understand why she's hurting all the time. The vet said it's all about quality of life. He said we'll know when it's time. She'll tell us, or we'll just know."

"I see," I said, but I didn't.

From that night onward I could barely look at the dog. I could barely even think her name. I knew she was dying, I knew she was going to die, and I knew there was no way to make her understand this but still I felt treasonous for not trying. I was sad for my mother too, and angry at her in strange flashes. How could a person spend years caring for another creature, keeping it alive, then one day take it all away? Sometimes I meant *how* like *how dare you* and other times I meant it like a real question, one I knew had an answer, one I knew my mother could give me, but I was afraid to ask. I was on the brink of real actual adulthood but I felt more like a child than ever. In bed every night I cried big fat helpless tears. My dog was dying, my childhood was ending, the rest of my life was beginning, and in a visceral way I felt that I wasn't cut out for any of it. I couldn't do what my mother was doing. I couldn't love anyone or anything the way she loved that dog, to say nothing of how much she loved me. She was so much like me, or I was so much like her, but in this way I believed she was some other type of person, one I was not and could not ever be.

One night in July she said, "It's time. It's just time." A few mornings later, my sister and I watched her settle the dog into a nest of blankets in the back of her Subaru and then my father drove us all to the vet's office. Later, I would remember so little, and so clearly. We walked from the car to the waiting room, from the waiting room to a small room down the hall. Someone carried the dog. Someone laid her on the table. We tried to all gather around but there wasn't enough room, or this is what I told myself when I stood behind my father. I saw nothing over his shoulders, heard only the vet tech's sympathetic murmuring, the tap of two glass vials set down on the metal table top. Something happened and something else, then someone said, "She's gone." But she wasn't gone, she was still there, she was just dead.

We left through a side door, waited by the car for a while, and then the vet tech emerged with a heavy bundle wrapped in black plastic. My father set the bundle in the back of the car, drove us home, then returned the dog to her pen for the last time. My mother followed him with a shovel. My sister and I followed her with nothing. My father began to dig and we all stood there and watched him. I closed my eyes for a long time and when I opened them again I expected to see a deep hole in the ground, but it was barely a shallow trough. "Woof," my father said, pausing to wipe his forehead, then began again.

My mother wandered off to water some flowers. My sister wandered off to lay in the hammock. I walked down the driveway to check the mail. Across the street, our neighbors were having a yard sale. They waved. I waved back. We had no mail. I walked back down the driveway. Now my mother was leaning against the Subaru with her arms crossed. I leaned next to her.

"You know," she said after a while. "I did this with Buster."

"Did what?" I said.

"I took him to be put down. Put to sleep. Whatever you

want to call it. I knew it was coming. I dreaded it. But I had to do it. He was my dog. I drove you girls to school then drove him to the vet and took him home. I buried him myself."

I had thought of that day plenty of times before—the shock of my mother's announcement, my dash up the stairs and down the hall and into bed, the beginning of my long refusal to see—but never what it must have been like for her. I watched my father across the yard still digging the hole, the black bundle at his feet. I tried to imagine my mother doing the same thing. I still didn't know where she'd buried him. "I just had to," she said again after a while, as if I'd asked her why or how.

Finally my father said, "Well, alrighty," and we all gathered around. He picked up the black plastic bundle and lay it down into the hole. My mother pulled the shovel up and began to fill the grave, dirt splattering against plastic bag, then dirt against dirt, until the earth was level with itself again. When we all left, she pulled the gate shut behind us.

* * *

The sable Pomeranian, who had papers declaring his name to be Putin Chang, had been adopted and returned to the shelter three times already by the time my mother's brother Tom met him and decided it was time for a fresh start. He took the dog home and named him Dutch. Dutch was intended to be a companion for Tom's aging Australian Shepherd, Tillie, a red merle with mismatched eyes, a wriggling shag ottoman. In general she projected an aura of beneficence, but she did not appreciate this gesture. The first time Tillie attacked Dutch, she managed to dislodge his right eyeball. The veterinarian who popped it back in said it should heal up fine, as long as it didn't happen again. When it happened again, Tom asked my grandparents if they wanted a roommate.

By the time Dutch came around, it had been nearly three decades since Nannie and Papa had a dog in their house. That was Daisy, the English Sheepdog; before, there had been a dachshund named Mona Lisa, and then Mona Lisa's son Freddie, the long, curly product of her liaison with a neighborhood poodle. In a photo of my grandparents taken before they were married, in the early 1940s, they're both kneeling and seem to be fully absorbed in the adoration of a fluffy creature identified on the photo's backside as "Trixie"; a photo from the same shoebox shows my grandfather's father and mother in similar formation around a black spaniel noted as "Inky." I imagine a procession of similar tableaus flipping backward through time, the human faces growing less and less familiar, the breeds increasingly obscure, only the posture between my ancestors and their dogs staying the same: *This one is mine.*

In my grandparents' dogless years, which happened to comprise my entire life up to that point, my grandfather had become a priest, retired from the priesthood, then un-retired and retired again so many times I lost track; my grandmother painted and quilted; they traveled to Hawaii and British Columbia and New Mexico and Ireland and France; they installed an above-ground swimming pool for their little grandkids then replaced it with a koi pond when we got big; they tended their day lilies and their blueberry bushes and their hydrangeas. Every other week, Papa mowed the grass of the steep front and back yards with his green-stained tennis shoes. For years, my mother begged him to outsource the job, certain he'd fall down the hill and break his neck. When he did fall, just before he turned 80, his neck was fine but his right arm ripped nearly out of its socket.

He got a new shoulder out of the ordeal, and a strange new fogginess. His hearing had been shot for years, blown out by machine-gun fire in the South Pacific, and we were all familiar with his tendency to turn down the volume on his hearing aids and float peaceably at the edges of busy rooms—say, anywhere that happened to contain all five of his granddaughters at the same time. But more and more he seemed confused about why he was in the room at all. By the time he was officially diagnosed with Alzheimer's, conversations with him had become nearly impossible about anything except the past. "At some point," my mother told me, "he'll simply stop making new memories." In time, that cutoff became clear: it was sometime in the spring of 2007, not long after his diagnosis, after my sister broke up with her first college boyfriend (whom Papa continued to inquire about, even after she broke up with her second college boyfriend) but before my college graduation (which Papa considered an upcoming event for the rest of his life). Everything else flowed like water through a paper bag. Except, somehow, Dutch.

Not long after my uncle installed the dog with my grandparents, I was up from Atlanta for the weekend and went with my mother to check in on the new trio, as she now did most days. Nannie met us at the door, waved us inside, and called for Papa, who soon emerged, beaming, followed close behind by what looked like a clump of something pulled from a larger creature's hairbrush. The clump was wheezing. "Here he is," Papa announced. "The little man!" Dutch ran in circles as we settled in around the living room, stopping briefly to surveil me with his one and a half eyes. After Tillie's second revolt, in a moment of extreme optimism, the vet had again popped the eyeball back into its socket. Now it was shriveled and withdrawn, rendering the dog perpetually mid-wink, like he was in on the joke that

204

was his life. He ran several more laps, jumped onto the couch, attempted to crawl up my mother's shirt, then leaped into my arms and extended his tongue up my nose halfway to my brain. He smelled like a stagnant pond in high summer. Then he tumbled to the floor and ran out of the room, his muddled breath crescendoing into a raspy *hork hork hork* that faded as he disappeared down the hall.

"He barely has a trachea," my mother informed me, quietly enough that Papa couldn't hear. "A perk of his high breeding."

Soon Dutch reappeared in the living room, carrying a cluster of twigs and dried leaves in his mouth. He deposited them at my feet with a flourish of drool. We all squealed and burst into applause. The dog took a victory lap around the coffee table then jumped into Papa's lap. "Oh, what a naughty little man!" my grandfather said, making no attempt to stop the long pink tongue from scrubbing every square inch of his face.

Whenever I came up for the weekend, my mother had a new warning for me before we saw Papa: "Don't mention the car—he and Frank had it out over the keys this week," or, "Talk loud—he keeps forgetting his hearing aids," or, "He's just really out of it lately." Sometimes he seemed better, sometimes worse. Sometimes he got talking about something that happened decades ago, and then it was like nothing had changed—he was the same version of himself I'd worshiped all those Sundays at church, teller of jokes and truths—then something would shift and he was gone again. And then I would be gone again, too, back to my life, leaving my mother to her own, which became increasingly dedicated to her father: the doctors' appointments begetting more doctors' appointments and the new prescriptions and the drug interactions and the skipped doses and the flares of anger and sadness and the general unspooling. One time

Papa called my parents in the middle of the night, panicked, saying he couldn't find Nannie anywhere. My parents drove across town in their pajamas and found my grand-mother sprawled on the grass halfway up the steep back-yard, bruises already oozing across her face. "What in the world were you doing back there?" my mother asked. But neither of them knew, or neither would say.

When my grandparents moved and/or were moved out of their home of five decades, it was first into an apartment on the upper floor of an Episcopal Church-affiliated "senior living community" downtown, where my grandfather repeatedly expressed regret that the windows were sealed shut or else he'd jump right out of them. Next it was into a new local outpost of a regional chain—called, incredibly, "Morning Pointe"—single-story, where the windows opened onto well-mulched flower beds and, even better, his desire for self-defenestration dissipated. My mother did her best to replicate the setup of their old living room in their new living room, down to the Pueblo pottery and Dresden figurines in the corner cupboard. What didn't come along was the dog. Tillie the Australian shepherd had recently accomplished her apparent goal of living out her golden years with my uncle all to herself, so the time was right for Tom to reclaim his prodigal ward. As a compromise, he drove Dutch across town to visit Nannie and Papa every week. The custodial arrangement was momentous enough to lodge in Papa's mind. Whenever I visited, he would ask me, "Do you know when Tom's bringing the little man to see me?" even when I'd just passed my uncle and the dog on their way out while I was coming in.

Tom began taking Dutch almost everywhere with him, often in a very small Harley Davidson-branded T-shirt and motorcycle hat. When Joe and I were planning our wedding, my mother told her brother, "Don't bring that dog to the wedding," but he did anyway, carrying the panting creature around in his arms all night, to the delight of our drunken friends. By then, Dutch's one good eye had gone bad and what little trachea he had was prone to collapse. It wasn't too long after that Tom had him put to sleep. He told Papa, then told him again and again, but this news never stuck. "If your grandfather mentions the dog, just change the subject," my mother advised me before my next visit. I knew it was the disease eating up his brain that was cruel, not me, but still I felt like a monster every time Papa said, "Do you know when Tom's bringing the little man to see me?" and I turned, instead, to my grandmother, and asked what they'd eaten for lunch.

* * *

Chester was a Boston Terrier, once black and white, now mostly gray. He was carried into the small room wrapped in blue blankets by a white-haired woman in a magenta sweatsuit. I did not know the dog, and I did not know the woman. I barely knew the veterinarian, about whom I was writing a profile for the university alumni magazine where I had become an editor. She had agreed to let me follow her around work for two days, taking notes. I'd watched her shave a Samoyed to better inspect his hot spot, diagnose a pit bull puppy with parvo, sedate a black lab so she could drain the giant hematoma on his ear, blood spurting when she pierced the taut skin. I'd watched her attempt to examine multiple cats who refused to emerge from their travel crates. I heard her say the words "you'll know when it's time" to at least a half dozen elderly creatures' human companions. Chester was her last patient on my last day.

"Chester," the vet said. "Chester, Chester, Chester."

The woman in the magenta sweatshirt lay him on the

207

metal exam table. His blankets fell away and underneath he was wearing a blue knit sweater. "It's time," the woman said. "He's telling me it's time."

I sat on a stool in the corner. The dog lay on the table, breathing shallow, looking at me. He had one eye, milky green. Grizzled fur grew over where the other should have been, a smooth dip in his skull.

The vet produced two glass vials and two syringes. "The first injection will make him sleep," she told the woman. "The second one will stop his heart." The woman nodded. She had big tears rolling down her face, which was as pink as her outfit. The vet asked, "Are you ready?" The woman nodded again, then put her arms around the dog on the table. The vet emptied one syringe into his flank, then the other, then said, "Now we wait."

So we waited, the woman and the vet on either side of the table and me on my stool in the corner. The woman slumped over the dog, shaking with little sobs. She had carried him into the room like a baby. I wondered if she thought of him as her baby, if she thought of herself as his mother. I imagined their life together: her darker-haired self holding him as a wiggling puppy, saying, "I think he's a Chester, don't you?" Her white strands creeping in over the years, and still her surprise when the dog's own face began to grizzle too. I imagined the years of daily routines, the walking routes, the spots on the couch permanently worn to the shape of their two bodies. What a hole there would be in her life tomorrow. What a hole there already was.

I thought that I remembered Sadie going quickly, but Chester kept breathing, an unhurried rise and fall. Kept breathing and kept staring at me with his one eye. I stared back. After a while the woman stood up, wiping her face. "This is stupid," she said. "So stupid." Just then, Chester began to pee. A long stream fountained up and arched across the room. The vet and the woman grabbed paper towels and scrambled around to sop it up. When the floor was dry, the vet turned back to the table and pressed her stethoscope to the dog's chest. "Okay," she said. "He's gone."

"Is he?" the woman said. She had stopped crying but now she began again. She unbuckled the dog's collar and peeled the damp sweater off his body. Then she pulled a tube of lipstick from her purse, applied it thickly, and kissed the dog's forehead. "Thank you," she said. I wasn't sure who she meant it for. Then she left. A tech came in and helped the vet slide the dog's body into a white plastic bag, which she carried to a chest freezer in the clinic's lab to await pickup from the local pet crematory. What a thing, I thought, to have the beloved companion of your life reduced to a handful of ash—their absence creating a new kind of presence. A few ounces of immortality, delivered one week later in a vial from Paws, Whiskers & Wings.

It was the end of a long day. The vet and the tech chatted as they set things to rights around the room—about Chester, about the woman in the pink sweatsuit, about her other dogs—and I listened, and I realized that I had been wrong. The woman had not met Chester as a puppy, had not named him, had not intertwined her life with his over many years. She worked with a Boston Terrier rescue organization to which Chester had been surrendered by his previous owners some months before. He had been old and sick; maybe they were old and sick, too—unable to care for him, I wanted to believe, rather than unwilling. At any rate, the woman had done what they could not or would not. From the collegial chit-chat I gathered that the woman had been in for several of these appointments in the past and would likely be back soon for another. Another bundle of blankets, another lipstick kiss on a forehead, another white bag in the freezer. She was right, it was so stupid. And she was stupid for doing it to herself over and over again. And I was so stupid because now I wanted it too.

* * *

The scruffy tricolor mutt arrived at the small-dog rescue center in Atlanta with no name and was being called Frodo when I met him, the Wednesday after the Sunday I convinced Joe that we should spend the following Saturday visiting shelters "just to see what's out there." I'd stopped by after work (might have left work early) to meet (just casually meet) a few dogs I'd seen on the center's website. I sat in a cubicle while the woman brought them to me one by one: Clancy, Rupert, Ally McBeagle. They sniffed my shoes, licked my hands, explored the small room's four corners. I liked them because they were dogs. They liked me because they were dogs. I was relieved, almost, not to fall in love. And then the woman said, "I've got this other guy—he's not on the website yet, he just came in yesterday." I followed her to a wall of metal crates. She unlatched one door, scooped out the dog, and handed him over to me, a mess of hair and skinny freckled legs that immediately began to thrash around until he launched himself out of my arms and skittered away down the hall. As if he was headed into oncoming traffic and not just the waiting room, I lunged after him, landing hard on the tile with, somehow, his tail in my hand: black with a white tip. He stopped and turned and looked back at me like, *Huh, okay.* His eyes were sad and wise. The woman led us back to the cubicle. I sat in the chair and said, "Do you want to be my buddy?" He jumped and put his front paws on my knees. By the time the woman came back with a handful of chopped hotdog for me to give him, he had jumped up and curled into my lap like a cat.

We got "Charles Darwin" etched onto his tag at Petco but we just called him Charlie. At first he slept so much I thought he was broken. He wouldn't eat unless we arranged the kibbles in a line on the floor. He seemed to like it when we sang to him, which was good because we couldn't stop. Any song could become a Charlie song. We lost our ever-loving minds. At first he wasn't allowed on the couch but then he was allowed on the couch. At first he slept in a crate at night but then he slept in our bed, under the covers, between us. Some mornings I woke with his head next to mine on my pillow. The shelter said he was a "terrier mix," but he turned out to be half purebred miniature poodle and half purebred beagle. A North Georgia puppy mill love-child, perhaps. Our poogle. *This one is mine.*

On his first visit to Chattanooga, a few weeks later, he was received like a visiting royal. Our mothers fawned, our fathers nodded approvingly. On the way into Morning Pointe to see Nannie and Papa, he left nurses and octogenarians swooning in his wake, though he didn't seem to notice—he pulled his leash taut, nose to the carpet, snuffling all the way down the hallway like he was hot on some trail. When I opened the door to my grandparents' apartment and Joe dropped the leash, Charlie ran straight to the couch, where Papa was sitting among the throw pillows. He saw the dog and his eyes lit up. "Well, would you look at that!" he said. "Where did you find him?" I told the whole story. When he asked again five minutes later—"Where did you *find* him?"—I told the story again. This was late March, 2014; he'd been sick for seven years. I was used to the routine, the repetitions, the recurrence. "Well, look at you!" he kept saying, running his hand from Charlie's quizzical brows to his white-tipped tail. "Look at you!"

The clock on the wall ticked toward their lunch hour. Joe and I stood to leave. Charlie, still on the couch next to

Papa, wouldn't budge. "Come on, stubborn beast," Joe said, scooping him up and heading to the door.

"I love you," I said to my grandparents as I stood to follow. "Y'all stay out of trouble."

"We'll sure try," Nannie said, like she always did. Papa didn't say anything. I wondered how long it would take him to forget we'd been there.

I was almost out the door when my grandfather bounced in his seat and turned toward me with a look of great urgency on his face, like he'd just remembered something so important. "Thank you!" he said. "Thank you for bringing the little man to visit me."

I realized then what he'd been thinking all along. *Where did you find him?*

"Oh, that's not—" I began, then caught myself. I didn't want to lie any more than I wanted to tell the truth, but what did it matter anymore? "You're welcome," I said. "He was glad to see you too." And as the door closed, the last thing I saw of my grandfather was the smile that split his face in two.

Here and There

One weekend every April, the nearly white sands of Orange Beach, Alabama, are swarmed by tourists, many of them drinking, some drunk enough to stand in a long line and pay ten American dollars to throw a dead fish over the state line into Florida. This event is called the Flora-Bama Mullet Toss. It is sponsored by an establishment called the Flora-Bama Lounge, a half-honky-tonk half-liquor store located half in Alabama and half in Florida. In 2014, when my friends rented a condo in Orange Beach for Mullet Toss weekend, our interests, like the Flora-Bama itself, were divided: half recreational, half anthropological. The plan was to go to the beach, drink beer, and people-watch all day, then go to the bar, drink more beer, and people-watch all night. We were all thirty or about to be thirty, all of us employed at various office jobs, mostly married or otherwise settled down, all the women eyeing each other to see who would have a baby first. Even those not chronically preoccupied with the inexorable passage of time had at least clocked that their hangovers felt worse than they used to. Nobody was saying it out loud but the trip felt something like a last blast before we were swallowed whole by our adult lives and whatever might come after.

The week before we were set to depart, on Easter Sunday, my grandfather had a stroke. Or maybe it was a bunch of little strokes, the doctor said the next day, he wasn't sure, but by then the specifics were unimportant. This would not be like the time he fell down the hill, or the time he had pneumonia, or the time they thought he had pneumonia but it was actually, somehow, a bladder infection. In Chattanooga, my mother and her brothers assembled at their parents' apartment at Morning Pointe, the ridiculousness of the name now fully acute. My father dispatched updates to me down in Atlanta. I told my friends that I might have to bail on the trip. I told myself that I would definitely have to bail on the trip. I waited until the last minute to pack, then called home to make sure I shouldn't change my plans. "Oh, no, honey, you should go," my mother said. "Papa would want you to." Was this true? How could this be true? But anyway, I went.

Ten of us caravanned down from Atlanta with our trunks full of Costco provisions. Our condo building, the Bella Luna, looked out over a marshy canal. Friday night, we ate sandwiches and drank beer and lounged around on the balcony. *Here I am at the Mullet Toss*, I kept thinking. *My grandfather is dying and I am at the Mullet Toss*. Maybe it did seem like something that he might think was funny. I imagined telling him the story one day, imagined how he'd laugh and say, "Land sakes!" As if that version of him wasn't already long gone. As if I might have the chance to tell him anything ever again.

Saturday morning, we set out early to claim our spots on the beach. My friends who tanned unfurled their towels and stretched out in the sun; I joined the freckle-and-burn crew under a giant pink-and-blue umbrella. We opened our books and the day's first beers. I was reading *The Secret History*. I liked that I knew on the first page who died and when and how, if not exactly why. I read one sentence, then read it again. I thought I heard my phone buzz in my tote bag. I pulled it out, but there was nothing to see except the clock and the picture of Charlie on my Lock Screen. I stuck the phone under my thigh and turned back to the book. I read the sentence again. My phone felt hot under my leg. I pulled it out and checked it again—nothing. I looked up and watched the waves slide in and out, milky green with brownish foam. The crowd was filling in now, closing in around us: neon string bikinis and American flag swim trunks, bare skin roasted and shining like Thanksgiving turkeys. A few of my friends stood, brushed the sand from their legs, and announced they were going to go toss some mullets. I waved them on their way. I felt my skin burning even in the shade. I checked my phone again—nothing, still nothing, just the dog and the minutes passing one by one.

That night, my friends went out to the Flora-Bama and I stayed behind. I made a gin and tonic. I took it and my phone out to the balcony. I drank the drink very slowly and watched for dolphins in the canal. The sky turned pink then purple then black. The dolphins never showed and my phone never buzzed. I went to sleep early and woke up early, not long after everyone else came home. I checked my phone—nothing. I wandered around the quiet condo, picking up empty cans. I checked my phone. I made coffee. I checked my phone. Nothing, nothing, nothing. I mimed a scream at the phone then threw it onto my rumpled bed, where it landed with no sound. I took my coffee onto the balcony and sat and watched the fog rise from the canal, a dirty white sheet stretching up to the dirty white sky.

I hate this, I kept thinking. *I hate this.*

I hated that my grandfather was dying, I hated that

we'd been losing him for so many years already, I hated that
there was nothing I could do, I hated my helplessness and
my superfluousness, and I was relieved by it, because I
didn't want to be there, really, I didn't want to see him
dying, I didn't want to see everyone else see him dying, and
I hated that too. And yet I had to do *something*, didn't I? So
all week I'd been wallowing in sympathetic misery, my own
vigil of sorts, a remote hyper-vigil, trying to keep the
thought of his death in the front of my mind—as if that
might protect me against the oncoming blast of its own
inevitability, as if just *thinking* might help anyone,
anywhere. The impulse was familiar. I'd done the same
thing in the weeks before Freddy died. Back then, I
attributed my angst to the specific circumstances: his age,
his denial of the diagnosis, his denial of the treatment, and
how the warped timeline of it all forced a reckoning with so
many denials of my own. Now, five years later, I thought of
myself as having accumulated a certain amount of fortitude
when it came to death—I'd gone to the funeral, I'd buried
the dog, I'd plowed ahead into my own life despite knowledge of the tragedy and horror that might await me—and
Papa was decidedly old, decidedly without options to
prolong his already-long life; this was, I thought, the best
way it could happen, the way it was supposed to happen,
since it had to happen at all. But I was still very very very
sad. Apparently, I'd thought it would somehow get easier.
Apparently, it did not get much easier. And it would only
continue. My grandfather was dying and then he would die
and then someone else I loved would be dying and then
they would die, and then another, and then another, there
would always be another. In a certain sense, I had always
been drinking coffee on a balcony over a dirty canal,
waiting for dolphins, waiting for someone to die. I had
always been straddling this invisible line, half among the

living, half among the dead. I had always been, and would always be, until that someone dying was me.

But it wasn't me, not yet. And so I drank my coffee and stared at the water, or the sky, or whatever it was. I finished my coffee and kept staring. I sat there long enough that my friends began to emerge from their bedrooms, woozy and chagrined. We were none of us in good shape but soon we were laughing. They debriefed me on the night before. Apparently there were clotheslines inside the bar where women hung their bras—skimpy lacy ones, padded beige ones—hundreds of them, maybe thousands, decades of accumulated lingerie. Land sakes! We made plans for day two. I resolved to rally. I would stand in the line, I would toss the mullet, I would go to the bar. The fog was gone now. The sun sparkled along the canal. Some dolphins finally cruised by. I forgot what I was trying to forget, and then I remembered. When I found my phone among my bedsheets, I had one missed call.

* * *

I hadn't been to my grandparents' old church in so long I was certain it would look nothing like I remembered, but it was somehow all the same: in through the big red doors and the cool, dim narthex to the dark nave with its blue tile floor, copper organ pipes, long wooden pews. The blue Books of Common Prayer were maybe even the same copies I'd pretended to read from as a child, mumbling along, understanding nothing. My mother and my uncles and grandmother took the first pew on the Epistle side, a row of salt-and-pepper curls. The rest of us filled in behind, my cousins and aunts and my father and my sister and her boyfriend. I sat between Joe and Marie, who had flown in from Utah, where she was living with her girlfriend Allison and a

217

border collie named Jeffrey Pine. I kept looking around for Papa, his white hair, his white robes, forgetting he was right there in front of us, on a pedestal set before the altar, a few handfuls of ash in a small wooden box.

Now there was another priest up there talking, a woman with auburn hair and purple cat-eye glasses. I remembered the pastor who gave Freddy's uncanny eulogy, and the pastor at Grandaddy's funeral who got my sister's name wrong, but this woman seemed to have known Papa, seemed to have loved him too. She stood up there and told the story of his whole life: Army recruit to insurance auditor to Episcopal priest, beloved youngest son to loving husband, father, grandfather. He was a sculptor, she said—something I had known, then forgotten, and now remembered again. When I was a child, he'd given me a small figure he carved from sandstone, a palm-sized hunched-over thing with a long nose. He said it was a flying monkey, like in *The Wizard of Oz*, but I didn't see it, couldn't grasp the abstraction. I was perplexed by the gift and unsure what to do with it. But I was proud, too, knowing that he was strong enough to make rocks take any shape he wanted, even shapes I didn't understand.

My uncles and mother rose to speak in birth order: Mike, Frank, Kathy, then Tom—leather jacket, bolo tie, ponytail. He took a deep breath before he began. "Years ago, my father and I had an argument," he said. "One of many. Something about politics, lightly heated. All other details lost to time. We hit an impasse, as we often did. But this time, this particular time, he handed me a tape and he said, 'I want you to listen to this.' So I went home, I took it home, and I played it like he said. I listened. And what I heard was a sermon he'd given at this very church on the Fourth of July some years ago. Sometime in the early nineties. We were on the verge of one international crisis or another, can't remember, take your pick. Anyway, I want you to hear what I heard that day." My uncle looked up and nodded. Somebody somewhere pressed a button and my grandfather's voice—his old voice, his younger voice—filled the room.

"In the name of God the father, God the son, and God the Holy Spirit, amen," he said. On the recording I could hear the sound of the long-ago congregation murmuring and settling in. "Well, happy Independence Day to all of you. The words of Jesus that we've just heard should force us to rethink some of our most basic reactions. 'Love your enemies. Pray for your persecutors.' Those are like bolts of lightning, breaking up comfortable patterns of thought and behavior for each one of us."

He said it again, slower now: "Love your enemies. Pray for your persecutors."

Each time he paused I could picture the line break on the page, I could see him sitting at his word processor upstairs at the old house, hitting the Return button once then twice.

"How un-American," he said. "How un-British. How un-French. You name the nationality—these words of our Lord simply do not carry much weight so far as nationalism is concerned, either ours or theirs."

Later I would figure out that he probably gave the sermon in 1993, the last time the Fourth of July fell on a Sunday before he retired from the priesthood for the first time. The New Testament reading must have been from the Gospel of Matthew. If I had been in the congregation that day, I would have been eight years old, feet swinging well above the floor.

"As a matter of fact," he said, "we've spent an enormous amount of energy developing and maintaining hatred for another people. And this is as much a preparation for war as the development of a munitions industry. This isn't to say that as a nation we're short on hate—God knows we're not short on hate. It's just that our hatred must be defined. It must be directed, loaded, and aimed, so to speak. So how does a nation train itself, or how is a nation trained—and more particularly, how does it prepare its fighting men to hate? Most of you know, but let me share my experiences of a period fifty-plus years ago."

He began to describe how, in the early years of World War II, the United States was coaxed out of its isolationism by months of nightly news reports, theaters full of war movies, and endless newsreels from the front lines. So when Japanese forces attacked at Pearl Harbor, he said, "We were now a nation psychologically ready for war, and war we would have."

"In 1943," he went on, "I was a high school senior. I had just turned seventeen that February. All during high school I had done whatever I could for the war effort—bought savings stamps, participated in scrap drives, anything I could do. My greatest fear at this time was that the war would end before I could serve."

A few days earlier, sorting through shoeboxes of old photos, my sister and I found one of him as a fresh recruit— dark hair, dark eyes, sharp jaw, big ears—and Sarah said, "Wow, he was a baby." I'd never put the dates together, never thought about how young he was. I'd rarely thought about that part of his life at all. I knew he'd done something with or near machine guns in the South Pacific, but my mother had relayed this information to me only begrudgingly, as an explanation for his use of hearing aids. "He doesn't like to talk about it," she told me, and so I diligently did not ask. In the absence of all other details, I'd always assumed that he'd been drafted, forced to serve, that some old bitterness drove his silence. I never imagined that he had yearned for war, craved it, obsessed over the possibility of joining the Army like I had over going to college, for some reason terrified that the chance would slip through his fingers.

"As my basic training commenced," he said, "and as part of the training and indoctrination, we were marched several times a week to the post theater where we saw Hollywood's gift to the war effort. It was called *Why We Fight*. And this series continued throughout our seventeen weeks of basic. As we saw in it, in living black and white, the rape of Nanking, the fall of Poland, the fall of the Netherlands, Belgium, France. And we all saw the latest from the Battle of Britain, which was still raging at this point. And we were given a good dose of the horrific scenes from Malaya, French Indo-China, Burma, and China herself. Our training at this point was designed to have the greatest appeal to boys like me."

I remembered a story about him walking out on a showing of *Thin Red Line*, his outright refusal to watch *Saving Private Ryan*. I remembered his repeated screenings of *Bedknobs and Broomsticks* for us grandkids, Angela Lansbury fighting Nazis with correspondence-course witchcraft. His helpless mirth at all episodes of *Fawlty Towers*, most especially "The Germans." *Don't mention the war!*

"I was full of ideas of my own immortality," he went on. "I was taught to do wondrous, exciting things with explosives. I learned to fire and maintain half a dozen weapons. And it was so exciting. It was really exciting. Just an oversized game. Best of all, I was away from home and didn't have my mama there to worry about me." He exaggerated his slight Southern drawl on "mama." In 1993, and in 2014, everyone chuckled. Then he said, "But now let's fast-forward our story to February of 1945," and everyone went quiet again. "The place is the city of Manilla. The war still seems like a game to me, but now I begin to understand how much damage a month of bombing and shelling can do to a large city. There are ruins all around me, and something else. The stench of burning flesh fills my nostrils and I realize that there are many people crushed under those piles of demolished and burning buildings. Now, I'm not aware of any immediate personal danger. But as I walk along, awed by this destruction, and just a bit sick at my stomach from the smell, I stumble over something. I look down. It's the body of a Japanese soldier, not long dead. I'm drawn to look at his face and I can see that he is young, no older than I am. There's a look of surprise on his face as he stares back at me through his sightless eyes. I am unable to tear my gaze away from his face. And through some trick of mind, I see my face in his face. And, my friends, that gave me goose-flesh. And it still gives me gooseflesh as I speak to you right now. Strange—"

He paused and I could picture it, his glance up and over the congregation, hand running along the raised hairs on his opposite forearm.

"I still shiver when I think about it."

Another pause, a breath, and he went on.

"At that moment, I became aware of my own mortality. And since that time I can't see a dead body or even think about death without still seeing that boy. For me, he came to symbolize all that is hateful in war, and the impossibly high price we pay for war. Here was the enemy, this Japanese boy I had been taught to hate and who I was sent halfway around the world to help destroy. I've forgotten many things in the nearly half-century since then, but I still have a crystal clear picture of that young Japanese boy, a son of Nippon, who didn't make it home to his mama. And the moment I saw that boy I found my hatred had left me. Life, I realized, was just too short to hate anyone."

He paused and sighed. "Well, the war in Luzon ended a few months later, and then in August, after the bomb—" Everyone around me sniffled and shifted in the pews as he continued, something about Korea and Vietnam, something about misgivings, something about a different way. But I was stuck back there in Manilla, hovering above that scene in the rubble, watching my grandfather stand there over the dead Japanese soldier, one boy staring at another, staring so long both of their dark heads turned gray then white and their bodies withered and sagged then fell into dust and blew away. And I seemed to blow away with them, or was lifted somehow out of my body, and I floated there above myself, up and to the right, staring down at myself and my family and everyone else who was gathered that day listening to the man who wasn't there.

"We do pray for the healing of ourselves and for those we love," I heard him say. "We do ask for guidance through prayer, we do pray for safety. Is it so far from reality for us to pray for our enemies? Are there limitations to what we can pray for?"

I thought of another sermon he'd given years ago, this one on Christmas Eve, which he began by asking, "What is today?" I was five or six, eager to please, especially him, and not yet familiar with the concept of rhetorical questions, and so I hollered from my seat, "IT'S *CHRISTMAS*, PAPA!" I felt the same pull now to respond to his questions, but far less confident about my answers. "NO!" I wanted to yell in reply. And then, "I GUESS NOT!" And then, "YOU KNOW, I'M NOT SURE IF I'VE EVER REALLY PRAYED, ACTUALLY? AND NOW THAT I THINK OF IT, MAYBE I NEVER ACTUALLY BELIEVED IN GOD, EITHER? MAYBE I ONLY EVER BELIEVED IN YOU?"

"As crazy as the idea sounds," he went on, as I

continued to float, "anyone who has prayed for an enemy can understand that this key teaching of Jesus is a very powerful experience. One that provides an enormous amount of resolution for our emotions, and actually quiets us physically by simply lessening the stress and releasing us from the destructiveness of pent-up anger and resentment."

"I WANT THAT," I wanted to yell. But who could give it to me? Who was my enemy? Who could I release to free myself? I thought of a few old bosses and a smattering of Republican politicians—a list so pathetic I almost laughed out loud, hovering up there above myself. Try again. I groped around in my mind, sifting through memory for any old clots of anger, shards of resentment.

"As a nation we might not be able to pull it off, but you and I could certainly do it," he said. "And consider this. When we realize ourselves by praying for our enemies and our persecutors, we're introducing another kind of force, another kind of power into the atmosphere. A power against which there can be no lasting resistance. Because love eventually wins the day, and Christ has proved this to us countless times."

Why was this so hard? Surely there was someone I'd lost sleep over, schemed against, railed against. Someone I'd longed to outsmart, outrun. Who had I wished to curse into nonexistence? Whose face would I most hate to see turn into my own? Who did I hate? But I couldn't see anything, no faces, no bodies, nothing at all, nothing but darkness, darkness, darkness.

And then it came to me, clear as black letters on a white page.

And then my grandfather said, "Let us pray."

In 1993, and in 2014, everyone bowed their heads.

"Oh God, the father of mankind, whose son commands us to love those who hate us, hear our prayer for our enemies. Lead them and us from prejudice to truth. Deliver them and us from deeds beneath the dignity of man. Turn us all from our evil ways. Take from our hearts every trace of cruelty, hatred, and lust for revenge. And in your good time enable us all to stand reconciled before you as friends of your son, our Lord and Savior, Jesus Christ," he said. "Amen."

"Amen," said everyone else, past and present.

"Amen," I said too, back in my body now.

Papa was gone, and now he was gone again. The service went on. We stood and kneeled and sat. We read the Apostles Creed and the Lord's Prayer and the Prayers of the People and the Commendation. The priest did one last blessing then took the box of my grandfather into her arms. The organ pulsed and the choir began to sing "Lift High the Cross" and she set off slowly down the aisle. My uncle Mike was next, pushing Nannie in the wheelchair she'd been nudged into for the day, then Frank and my mother and Tom. When I stood and turned to follow them I saw for the first time that the nave was full. I saw Joe's parents and friends of my parents, old friends of my uncles, more-wrinkled versions of faces I recalled from the same pews from childhood, and they were all watching us as we made our way down the aisle, pew after pew emptying in our wake.

The organ was blaring, the choir was singing, Papa's voice was ringing in my head, and it all harmonized into something, not a prayer exactly, it was more like the hot black orb that used to come visit me to say *you're going to die you're going to die you're going to die*, only now it said *I love you I love you I love you I love you*. And instead of death talking to me, I was talking to death—because this was my enemy, not a who but a what. It was death that I'd hated all my life, death who I'd been taught to hate, death who I feared and faced and feared again. Death who brought us here and death who would take us all away. It was death who I was conscripted to love. I remembered the sandstone monkey, the way it unnerved and impressed me, how I didn't want it and didn't know what to do with it. I didn't want this either. But I knew, at least, what I had to do.

At the far end of the nave, ushers held open the doors into the narthex. I followed my family toward and through like I'd done so many times before. Two more ushers held open the big red doors to the outside, the darkness of the anteroom suddenly framing a bright rectangle of the world: spring green, high sun, no shadows. The trunk of a live oak that had been growing longer than any of us. Out there, down the path, was the memorial garden where we would bury my grandfather's ashes under a Japanese maple. But here we stopped. I looked up, past my husband and cousin and sister and father and mother to see my uncles negotiating my grandmother's wheelchair over a raised threshold. It seemed right that we couldn't leave this place so easily. But then the wheel was free and our procession continued, each of us following whoever went before, blinking as we stepped out into the light.

The Beginning Again

Joe and I flew to Iceland as that summer became fall, right on the edge of the endless days and the endless dark. Upon arrival we were stupefied by jet lag, our brains goofy dark sludge, unsure where or when they were meant to be. At the rental car office outside the Keflavík airport a very blond man assigned us to a Subaru. "When you open the car door, hold tight," he said with a smile. "It is unlikely that you will hit another automobile on the roads here, but the wind will take the door right off its hinges. You must be careful. Will you be fording any rivers?"

"Hmm," Joe said. "We hadn't planned on it."

"Well, Iceland is full of surprises!" the blond man said, smile widening. "Just do not take the car through water any more than knee deep, okay?"

"Yes sir," Joe said, and took the keys.

Out on the highway, heading north to Reykjavík, it became apparent why it was so unlikely that we would hit another car: There were almost no other cars to hit. Beyond the flat snake of asphalt I saw little evidence of human life at all. On either side of us, fields of crumbled lava rock stretched toward a smothered horizon. Occasionally the silhouette of a house showed itself through the mist, but each time it felt like a trick. Massive black cairns rose up here and there, the stacked stones seeming larger than any human should be able to lift. I kept thinking I saw them move.

Somewhere to the east, a glacier-scabbed volcano named Bárðarbunga had recently begun to erupt for the first time in over a century. It started with a swarm of earthquakes under the ice, which opened up oozing fissures and let loose a hot, slow spread of lava along the glacier's northern edge, and then it began to bubble and roar. I had not been aware of Bárðarbunga in July, when I started to plan this trip as a celebration of my upcoming birthday. I was going to turn thirty in November and I was craving something new, something like a voyage into the unknown, though not so unknown that at least three friends couldn't email me tips from their own recent visits. I booked the tickets and promptly braced myself, as I had learned to do, for some strange event to compromise my plans—an act of terrorism, a national protest, a stroke. News of the volcano came right on time.

In the weeks before we were supposed to fly out, I tracked Bárðarbunga's progress as if it was spouting from our own backyard. I found a live webcam and kept it open in a browser tab at work, obsessively and then mindlessly clicking over to study the hot orange froth like it might hold some clues about my future. I remembered how, in 2010, the volcano under an ice cap called Eyjafjallajökull had sent up a miles-wide ash cloud 30,000 feet high and clogged trans-Atlantic air travel for a week. I read about how, in the late eighteenth century, a series of eruptions from the volcanic fissure Laki hurled plumes of hydrofluoric acid and sulfur dioxide into the atmosphere, first killing half of Iceland's livestock and decimating most of its crops—sending the island into a famine that starved perhaps a quarter of its population—then seeping outward to flummox global temperatures, drying up monsoon season across Africa and Asia, plunging North America into a summer of unsettling cold, and so thoroughly poisoning harvests across Western Europe that the resulting poverty may have hastened the French Revolution. And yet, as Bárðarbunga threatened to rage, I'd seen more thorough reporting in advance of snow flurries in Atlanta. Where was the round-the-clock news coverage, the meteorologists with their charts and maps and smug prognostications? The earth was exploding! Insides were becoming outsides! Would we die if we went on our trip? Would we die even if we didn't? Couldn't anyone tell me anything? Why were all 327,386 residents of this Kentucky-sized island in the North Atlantic treating this like it was nothing?

It was not until we were there on the ground that I began to consider that perhaps the volcano was being treated like nothing because it kind of *was* nothing. Or rather, it was something about which there was nothing to do. Volcanoes are not just prolific in Iceland; volcanoes *are* Iceland. There are at least a hundred and thirty of them, categorized into thirty-two systems, only thirteen of which are known to have been active since humans began living on the island in the late ninth century. Sometimes they send up poisonous ash clouds, sometimes they wash out highways and bury whole villages, and sometimes they just rumble and shimmy and go back to sleep for a hundred years. Their activities can be observed and predicted, up to a point, but they cannot be controlled or contained. Iceland is used to this. Iceland lives with this. It is simply the risk of being itself.

And now we were there. Here. We made it. We drove for a long time in silence.

"Hey, wait," I heard myself saying after a while. "Whose knees?"

"Whose knees what?" Joe said.

"The guy said don't drive through water more than knee-deep," I said. "But whose knees?" I was unable to articulate my sudden concern that Icelandic knees might be a unit of measurement distinct from American knees.

"Dunno," Joe said, yawning and shaking his head like a dog. "Maybe that's one of the surprises?"

* * *

In Reykjavík I could breathe again, the bright tin-roofed buildings and cobblestone streets sufficient proof that we hadn't dropped down onto a distant planet of evil rocks and fog. Hoods up against an intermittent drizzle, Joe and I meandered from our rented apartment into the city center where we knew there was a small lake but where we were still surprised to find a small lake. Couples strolled along its tidy, man-made banks; women pushed black prams with pink-cheeked babies dozing under plastic rain shields; old men fed birds. Across a footbridge, we came upon a black cinder block wall surrounding a handful of acres crammed with more trees than we'd seen on the whole drive up from the airport. We followed along the wall until we came to a wrought-iron gate. Beyond it, among the trees, gravestones shimmered in the rain. We went inside.

In the cemetery, everything was green and black except the yellow falling leaves. We walked up and down the rows, marveling over the inscriptions—Jon Barni Petursson, Ingibjorg Þorsteinsdóttir, Gundmund Gundmundsson—rolling the sounds around in our mouths, relishing the names like they were those of old friends, though we knew nothing of these people except when they were born and when they died and what their fathers were called. All these dead sons and dottirs, all their invisible mothers, ghost lines running back through time. Back home, Joe and I lived near a big old cemetery where we often took long walks, first just the two of us and later with the dog. It was sprawling and hilly and looped by a wide, shadeless driveway; there were always other dog-walking couples, and joggers, and neighborhood kids cutting through on their bikes to visit the nearby city pool. Our cemetery, as I thought of it, seemed not exactly alive but perhaps a bit oblivious to what it really was. But still there were people under the ground and stones above it, and I could move myself through them, I could read their names and dates, I could walk home with my heart still beating: *Not me, not yet. Not me, not yet.* Our walks there felt normal to me, an unremarkable fact of my life. But occasionally I did step out of myself a bit and marvel at how this was something I liked to do, indeed would choose to do, even on vacation partway around the world.

In this cemetery, in that cemetery, I thought often of my sister. The year before, I'd written an essay about my earliest encounters with death—the cemetery across the street from our school, our dead pets, our dead grandfather —and my impulse, in those years, to flee from those realities, versus my sister's inclination to turn herself toward them. The essay had begun another year earlier, that night at the bar, when my friend Kate said, of death, "I don't know, I've never really thought about it before," and I said, "Tell me what *that's* like." Before the essay was published, I emailed my sister a draft to read. Did she remember what I remembered? What had she made of it all? "I think I felt the same way towards the cemetery as I did towards nature, I guess?"

she wrote back. "It was a friendly thing for me, in kind of the way kids have imaginary friends. Like, a running internal dialogue with The Sublime? Ha? Not to say that I was never afraid of anything, but I think I felt a great deal of sympathy to and from, I don't know, The Spheres. The bigness of things when I was little was comforting to me, not frightening, and that was how I navigated loneliness. For a while I thought of all of that as being God, because I figured I was supposed to and what else could people be talking about, although that never really felt quite right to me. I guess the way death factored in to all of that was that whoever or whatever was dead I figured got absorbed into everything else, and that wasn't scary to me. Not that it wasn't confusing or sad or upsetting—the finality of death was difficult for me to understand because I still felt like I had access emotionally, so the realization of actual physical absence was sometimes pretty jarring to me. I don't know if that makes sense." But it did, more than most things ever had.

In Reykjavík, beyond the trees and walls of the cemetery, the rain stopped then started then stopped again; inside it, we were mostly shielded by the birches but occasionally subject to great shuddering cascades whenever the wind blew through the wet branches. Little yellow leaves came down over the living and the dead. I stopped on the path to adjust my layers and Joe said, "Stay right there, babe." He took a picture as I flipped my hood up over my head, a halo of fake fur. When he showed it to me later I looked sad but I knew that I was happy. Just to be there, alive, amid the bigness of things, with him.

* * *

On the far side of the cemetery was the National Museum of Iceland and inside the museum was an exhibit on the history of the island from its settlement in the late ninth century to its separation from Denmark in 1944. Apparently, the first Icelanders—Vikings, and likely their slaves, from Norway and the British Isles—would have seen not the lunar desolation that greeted us at the airport but land teeming with birch trees, countless acres of them, low and curly, ideal for roof-beams and firewood. So ideal, in fact, that the Vikings would end up nearly decimating them in a few hundred years' time. The trees they did leave standing had lived and died and decomposed a millennium ago, but a few pieces of settlement-era birch remained, naturally preserved long enough to be dug up and unnaturally preserved in a temperature-controlled glass box, their long-ago extraction conferring an ironic immortality.

Some bits of the Vikings themselves remained too. In one corner of the exhibit hall, the floorboards gave way to a translucent slab, under which lay two skeletons, an adult and an infant, each curled on their side. I edged around a scrum of jostling British teenagers to read the corresponding plaque. It said that archeologists had removed the pair from a burial site on the Reykjanes peninsula, near the Keflavík airport. They had died sometime in the tenth century; the adult, a woman, was around forty and the baby was about eight months old. Boy or girl, the plaque didn't know. Was the woman the baby's mother? The plaque didn't know that either, nobody did, nor how they died, though the baby's skull had been crushed, by death or by time.

Nearby, a glass box displayed a handful of items found buried alongside the woman in her grave: brooches and pins, an iron comb, a clam-shell spoon, a knife with a long-gone wooden handle. "Women were buried with jewelry and various cooking utensils, and tools for wool-working and other domestic tasks," the plaque said. "It is unclear, however, where they were expected to perform these duties in the next life." The plaque referenced a display across the hall, the remains of a Viking man buried with his horse. "According to the old religion, men who died in battle joined the god Óðinn in his great hall Valhalla. Those who died in their beds had to settle for eternity with Hel, the goddess of death. No indication is given as to where women went after death." Nothing had been buried along with the baby, or at least nothing that remained. "Children," the plaque said, "are not mentioned in sources on life after death in pagan beliefs."

I stood and stared down at the woman and the baby for a long time. I thought of Papa reading his own eulogy at his funeral a few months before, remembered him remembering how he stood and stared down at the dead Japanese soldier on the street in Manila, how he watched the boy's face turn into his own. I waited to see if something like that might happen to me now. The woman was almost too small to imagine as myself, she was more like a child, and the baby was her doll, one she never wanted but took into her arms anyway, unsure what else to do. I did not see my face in hers but I did feel her there, just under my skin.

Across the hall I found Joe standing and staring into a case of his own. It contained a palm-sized bronze figure of a bearded man sitting in a chair, grasping with two hands the handle of a tool. Joe turned to me with his eyes gleaming. The first Icelanders were mostly Norse pagans, he had just learned, who in the tenth century felt increasing pressure to conform with the culture of medieval Europe. Catholicism was the state religion by the year 1000, surpassed around 1550 by Lutheranism, and the rest of the exhibit was crowded with proof: wooden screens and staffs and big leather-bound books, many many delicately carved crowns of thorns. But this tiny bronze guy was less decisive. The tool he held was a hammer, but it was maybe also a cross. He straddled two worlds, unready to embrace or deny either one.

"Thor Christ," Joe said.

"Thor Christ!" I said.

"So metal," Joe said.

"Like, literally," I said.

Back at the apartment that night, as we crawled into bed, a band at a bar down the block started to play Tom Petty's "American Girl." Joe noted the irony and then began to snore. I lay next to him, staring into the dark. I was still thinking about the Vikings, the skeleton woman and baby laying across town in their own unfamiliar bed. It was dark where they were too, but quiet, all the tourists gone. I felt a surge of stupid concern: Were they warm enough? Were they lonely? I thought about them and their uncertain afterlives. I wondered what the Vikings considered a child and when they would say that child had become a man or a woman. I wondered how many years a boy would get before he began to fear dying in his bed more than dying in battle. I wondered when a girl would learn her fate of nothingness. I wondered if the woman died quickly or if she had time to think about where she was or wasn't going. Had she resented the men she knew for having a chance at glory, for being buried with their horses while she got stuck with a baby that may or may not have been her own? Did she have her own idea about what might await her on the other side? Did it help? And I wondered if it would have been a relief to her, the idea of Christ already creeping across the sea, that promise of redemption and life everlasting. Forgetting, in my wondering, all the ways it never felt like relief to me.

* * *

The sun showed itself as we were driving out of Reykjavík. North of the city everything was blue and green and gold, the land crumpled and creviced, piled up and eaten away. Mountains rose from great flatness then disappeared into fast-moving clouds whose shadows moved like herds of ghosts over the earth below. Every so often we passed a house, a barn, a gas station, but mostly it was miles and miles of no humans, only sheep, hundreds of dirty white puffballs grazing along electric green hillsides and galumphing away when we dared to interrupt their unhurried highway crossings. Every now and then, a rainbow shot through the sky.

"What *is* this place?" I kept asking, cackling in the passenger seat.

"We've died," Joe said. "We've died and gone to Super Mario World."

We drove north for a while and then west. The rain descended again as we crawled along the underside of the Snæfellsness peninsula. To the right of the highway hunkered Snæfellsjökull, a glacier-topped stratovolcano, this one inactive for a couple thousand years, now obscured by soupy clouds. Joe followed signs for an overlook with a view of the basalt crag formation called Lóndrangar. "Remember what the guy said," he said, and I did, but I didn't quite believe it until I opened my door just a crack and felt the wind grab at it like an overeager valet. The wind pulled us from the car, pushed us across the empty gravel parking lot, knocking our hoods back and plastering our faces with happy grimaces, nudging us along a path up a wet green knoll before chasing us down the other side. The path continued along the cliff's edge, which was bordered by a little gray rope strung along a line of thin metal stakes. I imagined pulling one and the entire line coming loose, like basting stitches, the whole cliff splitting and pouring into the sea.

The fog was thinner down here but the wind was stronger, rushing at us from above and behind and ahead and below. I grabbed Joe's arm and we hunched along the path until we could see the outline of the rocky cove and, across the way, Lóndrangar rising from the shoreline like an ossified horse. I couldn't stop laughing. On the path where the cliff elbowed into the cove, I took a few steps on my own and peered over the edge: a two-hundred-foot drop into freezing, frothing whirlpools and jagged basalt. The water was black, the rocks were black, but where they met was pure white foam, and in that moment I could see clearly how if we fell our bodies would smash against the rocks and our blood would briefly stain the whitecaps pink before the sea sucked us down whole, and we would be gone but this crashing, this pounding, would go on and on and on. A chill erupted in my extremities then rushed inward, gathered in my chest, and plumed up into my head. I felt like I was disintegrating. Something down there wanted me dead, I could feel it. It was pulling at me, whatever it was, and the wind was helping it, coming at me with mean, wet slaps. I scurried back to Joe, still laughing, giddy rollercoaster screams, the wind snatching every sound from my mouth.

"WHAT?" Joe yelled.

"WHAT?" I yelled back.

"WHAT?" we stood there yelling back and forth, clinging to one another, until I said, "LET'S GO!" And we turned and ran up the hill and down the other side and back to the safety of the car, breathing hard, wind slamming the doors behind us.

We drove on to Hellnar, a coastal village with a single hotel built on a cliff at the foot of a black-pointed mountain. That night, Joe fell asleep as soon as the lights were off. I lay staring into the dark, listening to the wind moaning through the eaves and the ocean muttering and thrashing below. When I closed my eyes, I fell into something that was not quite sleep. I found myself standing at the edge of a cliff, which faced another cliff. The wind was pushing at my back and gravity was pulling at my feet and the cold dread was rushing into me again, but when I looked over the edge I didn't see water and rocks a hundred feet below. I didn't see that, I didn't see anything. It was just nothing, and then I was falling into that nothing, falling all the way down into who knows what. I had enough time to register one thought —*Oh, so this is it!*—before I snapped back into myself, awake and alive, gasping in the dark, Joe snoring beside me, wind outside blowing like it hadn't stopped in a thousand years.

* * *

The mountains of Iceland were nothing like ours at home, the southern foothills of the Appalachians, where Tennessee's slumping Cumberland Plateau and gracious Blue Ridge peaks stumble down into Georgia's eerie monadnocks, where everything had been settling into itself for three hundred million years by the time what would become Iceland started fuming out of the North Atlantic. Here the land was young—raw, adolescent—which made it seem ancient. On that bleary drive from the airport the landscape had seemed dead to me, but up close it was resolutely, stubbornly alive: the last holdouts of summer's wildflowers and the first gold leaves of fall, wind-rumpled expanses of tawny grass, miles and miles of crumbled black rock, Laki's former insides, now centuries-cooled and smothered in pale green moss. *Bloom where you're planted,* I thought, but who had planted all this? The land had made itself, but where did the first spore of moss float in from, or the first birch catkin? How had any of us wound up here? Joe and I had paid for our tickets and tracked our plane's progress across the ocean on a little seat-back map and even our presence felt like a mystery.

From Hellnar, Joe and I drove north then east then south then east again, to Hveragerði and later to Vík. The parking lots were full at the famous waterfalls and the crater lake and the geyser named Geysir, but in between it was easy to imagine ourselves as the sole human occupants of the island if not the whole planet. We wandered around fields and empty old churchyards and along frigid streams and the edges of cliffs that looked just like the cliff I now saw every night when I closed my eyes, and Joe knew it, and he stepped always closer to the edge, laughing as I backed away cringing. Shaggy horses trotted up to greet us over wire fences, like we were as novel to them as they were to us, though probably they were just hoping for food. Joe and I would go for a long time without speaking real words, just grunting and gesturing. I took picture after picture, because like always I was afraid of forgetting, but here especially I didn't trust my own memory to account for what I'd seen. I could barely believe it all; why would anyone else? I felt in some moments that I might be losing my mind. In others, I felt reduced to some basic elements of myself, carbon and emotion, wonder and terror, flashing like a leaf before a storm.

When it started to rain or we got too cold or we just couldn't take it anymore, all the otherworldly earthiness, we'd run back to the Subaru and just sit there laughing. All interiors felt newly precious: the gas stations where we ate pylsur, the bars where we drank thin gold beer, our little hotels where every night Joe fell right to sleep and I tried my best to follow. Every night my body was dog-tired, ready to let go of the day, but my brain lodged its typical protest.

Every night I had to go to the cliff again. I had to walk to the edge and look over the edge, and I had to fall over it, over and over. It never stopped, and it never stopped feeling so real, but it did change. The first few nights it was just me. Then one night Joe was there, and we fell together. And then one night there was a baby. Once I might have been disturbed by any baby in any dream, but now its presence didn't bother me, only how I had to watch from above, help-less, as it crawled to the cliff's edge and fell over too.

* * *

One day we drove west from Vík until we saw a glacier oozing down a black mountain into a wide lake the color of milky tea: Jökulsárlón. Icebergs as big as cars, as big as houses, were doubled in the trembling mirror of the water. Most were far off, tinged blue, drifting imperceptibly, but as we walked along we came across one chunk that had beached itself on the gravelly shoreline. I felt an odd pang when I saw it, as if it had once been an alive thing, like one of the seals whose slick black heads kept popping up out of the water, and here it had met its undignified end. It looked as if it had been dumped from a cooler at the end of a cook-out. I nudged it with my boot and a bit crumbled off. Just ice, dirty melting ice.

Joe picked along the shore and I followed him and the pang followed me too, gathering into the pressure of a new but not-unfamiliar sadness. It was similar to a sensation I'd grown accustomed to back at home, a vague feeling upon entering a place that something bad once happened there, like how I'd felt passing by the Old Slave Mart on our long-ago carriage ride in Charleston, and staring into the hole in the ground in Manhattan, and looking out across the field at Gettysburg: something human made inhumane, something

240

precious spoiled. It was similar, also, to how I'd felt the first time I saw a sunset after somebody at school said the reason sunsets are so beautiful is all the air pollution, and how I felt when the mercury said 72 degrees, my ideal outdoor temperature, but the calendar said Christmas Eve—the sense that I was encountering beauty at some great cost.

Later, a Google search confirmed my hunch: Jökulsárlón had not existed until 1935, when the glacier above it—Breiðamerkurjökull, an offshoot of Vatnajökull, the largest icecap in Iceland and the second-largest in Europe—began to melt, the runoff collecting in a convenient bowl of earth. Over the course of eighty increasingly warm years it had become Iceland's deepest lake, growing as the glacier shrank. I did not know it then, but glaciers can die too. Earlier that year, in fact, an Icelandic glaciologist had determined that a glacier named Ok, which lay across a volcano northeast of Reykjavík, had lost too much mass to be considered a glacier anymore. It was not quite *gone* but it was no longer sufficiently *there*. In 2019, a few hundred Icelanders would gather for a funeral for Ok and leave behind a bronze plaque affixed to a stone that had been revealed by the retreating ice. "Ok is the first Icelandic glacier to lose its status as a glacier," the plaque would say in Icelandic and English. "In the next 200 years, all our glaciers are expected to follow the same path." The plaque would also list a date, "Ágúst 2019," and a measurement: "415ppm CO2." Four hundred fifteen parts per million, the level of carbon dioxide then present in the Earth's atmosphere. Climate scientists took the reading earlier in 2019 from atop a volcano in Hawaii, the highest level yet recorded. Five years earlier, in 2014—the year of Ok's death, the year of our visit—it had been 397.2ppm. Five years later, in 2024, it would be 424.61ppm. By then, each of the past ten years would have been the warmest year on record. "This monument is to acknowledge that we know what is happening and what needs to be done," the dead glacier's headstone would also say, addressing an unknown reader in an uncertain future. "Only you know if we did it."

* * *

In Vík we stayed at the Hotel Volcano, where sheep prowled in the grass outside our window and a map of Iceland covered one wall of the lobby. On our last morning, Joe and I stopped to retrace our meandering routes. The shape of the country was familiar by now, the bristling body with one long arm and a frantic, screaming head. We'd only been there nine days but it felt like forever, like we must have covered the whole of the island, though now I realized how much we hadn't seen.

The hotel was marked on the map with a star. All the volcanoes were marked with triangles. "Look, here's Bárðarbunga," I said to Joe, the first time I'd thought of it since the day we landed, after weeks of thinking about it constantly. "And here's ol' Eyjafjallajökull."

The hotel owner walked by just in time to hear me absolutely butcher the name. "Yes, our local celebrity," he said with a smile.

"It's so close to the hotel," Joe said. "Was it bad here when it was erupting?"

The owner shrugged. "Not good, but we've seen worse. The one we worry about is Katla, right here." He tapped a triangle even closer to the hotel. "Usually after Eyjafjallajökull erupts, Katla goes too. But she hasn't blown since 1918. We are long overdue. When she goes next..." He shook his head. "Katla is under a glacier, this one here, Mýrdalsjökull. The lava flow will not reach us here in Vík, but the flash floods from the melting ice will. It will be

242

water and ash all the way to the sea." He moved his hand like he was brushing crumbs off a table. The three of us stood there staring at the map for a while, silent. Then the hotel owner clapped his hands together once and said, "Well! I will let you get on with your morning. You have had a nice stay, yes?"

"Oh, yes!" Joe said brightly and I said, "Yes, wonderful, thank you!"

"Good, good!" he said and disappeared down the hall.

We left the hotel and drove west out of Vík. As if to make up for lost time, some kind of penance, I made myself imagine a hot gray wave coming down from the frozen mountains to the north, a torrent of sludge smothering hills and cliffs and sheep and horses, snuffing out waterfalls, smudging out the Hotel Volcano and the whole town as it poured itself into the sea, all of it lost forever except to the curious diggers of the future. What would they think when they tried to piece it all back together? How would they say we lived, what we believed, where we thought we were going when we died? Then I thought about the ninth century, and I thought about the twenty-first, and I thought about the thirty-second, and I just laughed.

We stopped in Reykjavík for the afternoon. The city had been a stranger the week before, but now it was the closest I'd felt to home in days. We planned to visit the Icelandic Phallological Museum then walk down to Bæjarins Beztu for our final pylsur, but the tanks of preserved whale penises sent us searching for a slightly less oblong lunch. We were walking down Klapparstíg when we came upon an old bookstore. At first I thought it was closed, the windows covered in sun-faded butcher paper, but Joe saw that the small sign on the door said "OPIÐ" so we went through.

Inside was a dim labyrinth of shelves packed floor to

ceiling with books of all languages and eras and genres arranged by no particular obvious logic. A gray-haired man sat behind the counter, head down, unbothered by our presence. Joe and I parted ways slowly, like we were afraid to upset the balance of the place. I made my way down one avenue of shelves, turned one corner, then another, and there I came upon a clearing. In the middle sat a wide, low table, stacked with stacks of books, like thirty years ago someone had been in the middle of shelving or unshelving and walked away and never returned. Then my eyes landed on one book in particular, the one atop the stack closest to me. It had a pale green linen hardcover, no dust jacket, the author and title stamped in darker green: Hans Liep, *Der Gross Fluss im Meer*.

It lay there as if it had been left out for me. *But that's impossible,* I thought. The book couldn't be there because it was on my shelf at home, in Atlanta, three thousand miles away. It was on my shelf in Atlanta because I'd bought it years ago at a used bookstore in Chattanooga, back when I was taking German in college, back when I thought I might get good enough to read a whole novel. Plus I liked the look of it; the spine bore some abstract midcentury squiggles it took me years to realize were meant to be boats. I got exactly good enough at German to translate the title: *The Great River in the Sea*. And it wasn't a novel after all, it was nonfiction, something about the Atlantic Gulf Stream. I kept it anyway. I moved it with me for the next ten years, packed and unpacked it from various boxes, set various houseplants upon it, never once cracking the spine. At some point I decided I owned the only copy in the world. But here was another.

I picked it up from the table and held it to my chest, the way I'd pick up anything that was already mine. I carried it around the store, up and down the narrow alleys of crime fiction and poetry and leather-bound tomes of old science and dead religion. I knew I was going to buy it, and I was filled with dread. Because if I bought this one then I'd have to buy them all, every copy of *Der Gross Fluss im Meer* I ever came across for the rest of my life, and if I found this one here then I knew I'd find one in every bookstore in every city I visited for the rest of my life. And I'd buy them all, I'd carry them with me, and I would learn nothing, no matter the cost.

After a while I found myself back at the table in the clearing. I stood there for a while, the book growing heavy in my hands.

Finally, Joe emerged across the way. His arms were full. "Find anything, babe?" he said.

I looked down at the book like it might tell me what to do. How strange, this desire to possess something simply because I'd possessed something like it before. This fear of letting go of what was never actually mine.

"Nah," I said, setting the book down among all the others. "Nothing I can't live without."

* * *

Back in Keflavík, the night before our early flight home, we ate dinner at a tourist bar on the marina: fried fish and a final round of pale, pale ales. At our hotel up the hill, our room was stuffy and the blanket was itchy and Joe was soon snoring, undaunted.

I was exhausted but fighting it like a child. I lay awake turning the week over in my mind, sorting and folding and stuffing the memories like I'd done to our duffel bags of dirty clothes that evening so Joe's armful of new old books would fit. I thought again of the Vikings from the museum, the woman and the baby, and I remembered they'd been buried and unburied not far from here, somewhere along the Reykjanes peninsula. At dinner we'd sat for a while, not eating, not talking, just looking out at the water, and I thought about how, minus the dining room's wall of windows, minus the town lights reflected in the waves, the Viking woman might have once had a similar view. I imagined her standing there on the shore with the baby in her arms, both of them staring across the distance of gray-blue water rolling out to gray-blue sky. I wondered if she knew what was out there, past where she could see, or if she knew that she would never know, and I wondered if that made her sad, or if that made her feel free, or if it was presumptuous or maybe just stupid to force all these questions on a woman so long dead. She must have had plenty of questions in her own time. Maybe she had answers too. That stuff they buried her with, maybe she did know where she'd use it. Maybe she didn't like the story she was told, so she told herself a better one. Maybe she gave herself Valhalla. Or maybe she let herself believe what the men wouldn't, that her life on this earth was the only one she'd ever know. That she wasn't going anywhere she hadn't already been. *Oh, so this is it!*

The day was coming to an end, the trip was coming to an end, the summer was coming to an end, the third decade of my life was coming to an end. I knew so much now and I knew so little. What would that Viking woman make of my existence, I wondered, any single part of it: the computer I sat before all day at work, the computer I kept all the time in my jeans pocket, the jeans themselves. The machine we'd just driven all around her island, seeing more than she might have seen in her whole lifetime. The bigger machine that flew us here, over the endless ocean. The antibodies pushed long ago into my blood, the daubs of silver amalgam blocking the rot of my teeth, the little plastic T recently threaded into my uterus giving me five to seven years to decide if I wanted a baby. (Had she wanted that baby? Was it even hers? Did it matter?) But the woman knew plenty that I did not: how to weave and start a fire, how to speak her craggy dialect, maybe even how to pray. And most of all she knew what happens when life draws to a point, its final point. The question I'd once asked my friend Kate, the question I would spend the next ten years asking myself, was the same question I now wanted to ask of the Viking woman, and my grandfathers and my uncle and all the rest. *Tell me what that's like.* To live and to die and then to be dead. They all know and I know that one day I'll know too, and I've never wanted anything more, and I've never wanted anything less—this maddening consolation prize, this best-kept secret, perhaps the only true secret, and always told too late. Or maybe just in time. Who can say? Not me, not yet.

I lay there staring into the dark until my mind slowed and blurred. Tonight, at least, I knew what was coming when I closed my eyes. It had become a nightly ritual, something steady in this strange land on this strange planet. I would stand again at the cliff's edge and then tumble into the unseeable dark. I would fall and fall and fall. Joe would join me there, and maybe the baby too, and we would all fall together. And all the while I would feel the black buzz of gravity shaking through my body, dark bubbles rising and popping in my brain, and I'd hang for a while on the edge of oblivion. Then the fear would pass and I would come back to myself, always back to myself, and finally I would sleep, and then I would wake, and wake and wake and wake again, until at last I came to whatever would be the end.

Acknowledgments

Thank you first to my family, who bear the memoirist in their midst with patience and good humor. My parents, Ralph & Kathy Maddux. My sister, Sarah Maddux (and Steven and Eula). My cousins: Marie Landis, Claire Davis, and Lucy Ellis, and Chris Landis and Jon Landis. My Landis uncles and aunts: Mike & Marcia, Frank, and Tom & Melissa. My aunt, Susan Maddux. And my in-laws, Pat & Susan McCormick and Jenn McCormick Nance (and Colby and Ostara).

I am grateful to the memories of my grandfathers, Sid Maddux and Richard Landis; my great-uncle, Fred Maddux; and my uncle, Freddy Maddux.

I am grateful also to my grandmothers, Mary Ralph Maddux and Martha Landis, and my aunt, Susan Landis, who all three died in the years I spent working on this book. Their lives shaped my own, and the stories I tell about it, in ways I barely understand.

Thank you to Abby Greenbaum and Hannah Palmer, my Argonauts, for your tireless eyes and brains and hearts.

Thank you to my steadfast Warhorse Witches: Kate Tuttle, Laura McKee, and Stacy Mattingly. And to Esther Lee, Melanie Jordan, and Suzanne Moses, and to the Goat Farm Arts Center.

I got my MFA in overthinking at The Marlay in Decatur, Georgia. Thank you to my Biblio Babes and the mafia booth.

Thank you, Duvall Osteen, for your confidence.

Thank you, Rebecca Bowen, for the untangling.

Thank you to the editors of *The Paris Review Daily* (Sadie Stein), *Pacific Standard* (Leah Reich), *Matter* (Leah Beckmann), *Guernica* (Hillary Brenhouse), and *Europe Now* (Kayla Maiuri) for publishing early versions of some of these chapters.

I am grateful to any friend who ever indicated their belief this book's eventual existence. In particular: Ally Van Houten, Aliza Lailari, Amelia Lerner & Lain Shakespeare, Austin & Erin Ray, Brooke Hatfield, Gray Chapman, Meghan Dahl, Meg Lindsay, Miriam & John Brown Spiers, Sarah Fierman, and Van Jensen. Thanks to Kate Kiefer Lee for the clarifying bewilderment. Thanks to Cindy Sullivan for the finger fib, and for your faith.

I wrote nine of this book's ten drafts in the company of a dog named Charles Darwin. He was illiterate, and now he is dead, but I'll say it anyway: Thanks, buddy. I miss you.

Most of all: Thank you to Joe, for everything.

And to Ramona, for everything and more.

About the Author

Rachael Maddux is a writer and an editor. Her essays and features have appeared in the *Oxford American*, *Virginia Quarterly Review*, *Garden & Gun*, and elsewhere. Her work has been noted in *Best American Sports Writing* (2016) and collected in *Best American Travel Writing* (2015). In 2010, she was a finalist for a National Magazine Award in Reviews & Criticism. After many years in Atlanta, Georgia, she now lives with her family in Chattanooga, Tennessee, where she grew up.

Also by Rachael Maddux

The Void: Notes On A Few Miscarriages

Third Person: Notes On A First Year